Department of Homeland Security
Federal Law Enforcement Training Center
Glynco, Georgia

F.L.E.T.C.

Legal Division

Practice Exams

(4th Amendment, 5th and 6th Amendments, Courtroom Evidence, Electronic Law and Evidence, Federal Court Procedures, and Officer Liability)

Homeland Security

SH - 1000

June 2009

FLETC Legal Division
Practice Exam Guide – June 2009

1. The purpose of the practice exams is not to give hints on the actual exam, but to help students learn how to apply legal principles in a factual situation.

2. This practice exam may not address all the EPOs you are responsible for, or all the materials you must know to master an EPO. The student is responsible for knowing and mastering the EPOs.

3. These questions may be harder or easier than the exam.

4. Students will find reviewing the answers - even the incorrect ones - will help them master the principles.

The Legal Division hopes this practice exam helps you.

Keith Hodges, Senior Instructor
Legal Division
(912) 554-4757, keith.hodges@dhs.gov

4th Amendment – Start on Page 1	
Program	**Questions**
CITP, Exam 1	1 - 11
CITP, Exam 3	12 – 32.
ICE-D, Exam 1	1 – 11.
ICE-D, Exam 3	12-32 except 19.
ICITP	1, 3, 4, 5, 6, and 7.
UPTP	All except 19, 20, and 27.
LMPT	All.
5th and 6th Amendments - Start on page 33	
CITP	All
UPTP, LMPT and ICE-D	1 – 12 only
Courtroom Evidence – Start on page 51	
CITP	1-4, 9, 12-17, 20-23.
UPTP and LMPT	1-4, 9-17.
ICITP	1-4, 9, 15-17, 20-23.
Electronic Law and Evidence – Start on page 64	
CITP	All
Federal Court Procedures – Start on page 81	
CITP	All except 32-33.
LMPT	All
UPTP, GSA-FPS	1-11, 36-39
ICITP	8-23, 27-31
ICE-D	1-9, 12, 16-17, 19-23, 25, 27-31, 35-39
Officer Liability – Start on page 100	
All	All questions except #9

Changes to June 2009 version of the LGD Practice Exam

The guide sheet was amended to reflect changes to questions for LMPT as the EPOs for 5th & 6th Amendments, Courtroom Evidence, and Officer Liability have changed.

5th / 6th Amendment, question 17 (CITP only). Typo fixed in distracters.

4th Amendment.

- The following questions were changed to reflect the change in SIA law pursuant to *Arizona v. Gant:* 17, 21, and 24.
- Minor changes were made to the following questions to improve readability: 15 and 28.

4th Amendment Practice Exam

1. Thompson is suspected of running a counterfeiting operation out of his garage. The garage is attached to the dwelling. Without a warrant, three officers step onto his curtilage, shine a flashlight into the garage, and take a quick look. They observe a number of what appear to be $100 bills hanging from a clothesline. With this observation, they attempt to secure a warrant. Their request for a search warrant should be -

a. Denied, because the officers intruded on a location where Thompson had a reasonable expectation of privacy without either a warrant or an exception to the 4th Amendment.

b. Denied, because the use of a flashlight violated Thompson's reasonable expectation of privacy.

c. Granted, because the garage does not have curtilage, in that it is not a dwelling.

d. Granted, because the garage itself was not within the curtilage of Thompson's dwelling.

---

a. Denied, because the officers intruded on a location where Thompson had a reasonable expectation of privacy without either a warrant or an exception to the 4th Amendment.
CORRECT: The root of the question says that the officers were on Thompson's curtilage. The officers did not have a warrant to be there and there is no 4th Amendment exception. The information they obtained in violation of Thompson's REP cannot be lawfully used to obtain a warrant.

b. Denied, because the use of a flashlight violated Thompson's reasonable expectation of privacy.
INCORRECT: Using a flashlight, by itself, does not violate a person's REP.

c. Granted, because the garage does not have curtilage, in that it is not a dwelling.
INCORRECT: Curtilage is not limited to dwellings and includes areas surrounding a dwelling. (Review your student text.)

d. Granted, because the garage itself was not within the curtilage of Thompson's dwelling.
INCORRECT: The garage was attached to the house so it was very likely on the curtilage. More importantly, the officers were unlawfully on the curtilage when they made their observations.

2. Agents develop reasonable suspicion that Wooster is operating a stolen credit card ring. Upon seeing Wooster driving in his car one afternoon, the agents follow him. When he arrives at a shopping mall, the agents approach him, identify themselves, and tell him to put his hands on his automobile. One of the agents frisks him and, in the upper left hand pocket, feels what is immediately apparent to him as a stack of credit cards bound by a rubber band. The agent removes the credit cards and, ultimately, determines that they are stolen. Wooster's motion to suppress the credit cards will be -

a. Denied, because the agents had reasonable suspicion of criminal activity.

b. Denied, because the agents had probable cause to remove the cards from his pocket under the "plain touch" doctrine.

c. Granted, because the agents performed an illegal "frisk" of Wooster.

d. Granted, because a "frisk" may result only in the discovery of weapons on a suspect.

---

a. Denied, because the agents had reasonable suspicion of criminal activity.
INCORRECT: The officers only had reasonable suspicion criminal activity was afoot which would allow them to make a Terry stop and direct Wooster out of his car. The officers did not have reasonable suspicion that Wooster was presently armed and dangerous making the Terry frisk illegal. The crime of operating a stolen credit card ring is not the type of offense which would give R/S a person is presently armed and dangerous (like one would have with R/S someone committed a robbery or burglary.)

b. Denied, because the agents had probable cause to remove the cards from his pocket under the "plain touch" doctrine.
INCORRECT: The Terry frisk was illegal. (See a above.) The credit cards were discovered during an illegal frisk. If the officers had R/S Wooster was presently armed and dangerous, they could have frisked Wooster. Even then the plain touch doctrine would not apply because it was not immediately apparent that the credit cards were stolen (just that they were credit cards.)

c. Granted, because the agents performed an illegal "frisk" of Wooster.
CORRECT: The officers only had reasonable suspicion criminal activity was afoot which would allow them to make a Terry stop and direct Wooster out of his car. The officers did not have reasonable suspicion that Wooster was presently armed and dangerous making the Terry frisk illegal.

d. Granted, because a "frisk" may result only in the discovery of weapons on a suspect.
INCORRECT: A lawful Terry frisk is a pat down of the outer clothing to look for weapons or hard objects that may used as a weapon. In a lawful Terry frisk, not only may the officer retrieve weapons, he/she may also retrieve hard objects that might be a weapon and soft objects that are immediately apparent to be contraband. (Review plain touch in your student text.)

3. Johnson is arrested for drunk driving and failing to pay child support. He agrees to share information with the police to avoid prosecution. Having been personally involved in every aspect of an ongoing stolen paycheck operation, Johnson explained the intimate details to the police of what he saw and did with Fred, a co-criminal. Based on his statements alone, the officers seek a search warrant for the co-criminal's premises where Johnson stated he saw many of the stolen checks the day before. The application for a search warrant will be -

a. Granted, because Johnson's statements amount to probable cause and the officers can meet the Aguilar standard.

b. Granted, because Johnson has never provided false information to the officers in the past.

c. Denied, because the officers did not corroborate Johnson's statements.

d. Denied, because there is no probable cause..

---

a. Granted, because Johnson's statements amount to probable cause and the officers can meet the Aguilar standard.
CORRECT: The information known to the officers show both that Johnson was reliable and had a basis of knowledge in what he told the officers. Because he is a co-criminal, the information he provided is presumed reliable.

b. Granted, because Johnson has never provided false information to the officers in the past.
INCORRECT: Even if true, this would go to Johnson's reliability. It would not, however, establish a basis of knowledge.

c. Denied, because the officers did not corroborate Johnson's statements.
INCORRECT: Because the Aguilar test was satisfied (reliability and basis of knowledge,) there was no requirement to corroborate the information.

d. Denied, because there is no probable cause..
INCORRECT: See answer a. The Aguilar test was met.

4. An officer is walking down a public sidewalk in the early evening hours, just after dark. Glancing in the direction of Sweeney's home, the officer notices that, while Sweeney has drawn the curtains in the front window, there is a gap through which the officer sees what he knows to be a large marijuana plant. The following morning, based solely upon this information, the officer seeks a search warrant for Sweeney's home. The request for a search warrant will be -

a. Granted, because the officer could have entered the home the previous evening under the "exigent circumstances" exception to the warrant requirement, and seeking a warrant is nothing more than a court order of the "exigent circumstances" exception.

b. Granted, because the officer did not violate Sweeney's reasonable expectation of privacy in making the observation on which the search warrant will be based.

c. Denied, because the officer's view into Sweeney's home amounted to an intrusion into a location where Sweeney had a reasonable expectation of privacy without either a warrant or an exception to the warrant requirement.

d. Denied, because the officer had no reason to look into Sweeney's home; the observation alone did not amount to probable cause; and the officer did not enter the home at the moment she made the observation.

---

a. Granted, because the officer could have entered the home the previous evening under the "exigent circumstances" exception to the warrant requirement, and seeking a warrant is nothing more than a court order of the "exigent circumstances" exception.
INCORRECT: The root sets forth nothing which would establish an exigent circumstance.

b. Granted, because the officer did not violate Sweeney's reasonable expectation of privacy in making the observation on which the search warrant will be based.
CORRECT: The officer was in a public place (where he had the right to be) and the open curtain exposed the inside of the house to the public. The homeowner had no REP in what he exposed to the street outside. Accordingly, what the officer saw in the window was lawfully obtained and can establish information that may be used in the warrant.

c. Denied, because the officer's view into Sweeney's home amounted to an intrusion into a location where Sweeney had a reasonable expectation of privacy without either a warrant or an exception to the warrant requirement.
INCORRECT: Leaving the curtain open and exposing the inside of the home to public view means the homeowner did not have REP in what he exposed to the public.

d. Denied, because the officer had no reason to look into Sweeney's home; the observation alone did not amount to probable cause; and the officer did not enter the home at the moment she made the observation.
INCORRECT: The officer does not have to have a reason to look in the window. Nothing prevents the officer - and a private citizen - from looking through the window while standing in a public place. What the officer saw did amount to PC. There is no requirement to immediately enter the house. In fact, even though the officer saw the plants and developed PC when he did so, he could not enter the house unless he had a warrant, consent, or an exigent circumstance.

5. Marsh checked a suitcase at the airline counter and got onto an airplane. Before the suitcase was placed on the airplane, it was sniffed by a drug detection dog. The dog indicated that drugs were located inside which established probable cause to search the suitcase. With this knowledge, two DEA agents entered the airplane, approached Marsh, identified themselves, and asked him if they could look in the suitcase he had checked at the counter. Marsh stated, "I'm not traveling with a suitcase." Because the plane wasn't scheduled to take off for an hour (and Marsh didn't think he would miss the plane), Marsh voluntarily agreed to accompany the agents to the suitcase, was shown the suitcase, and was asked again if they could open it. Again, Marsh denied ever seeing the suitcase. The agents opened the suitcase and discovered contraband inside. At trial, the contraband should be -

a. Admitted, because the officers had probable cause to search the suitcase.

b. Admitted, because Marsh abandoned the suitcase.

c. Suppressed, because the officers violated Marsh's reasonable expectation of privacy.

d. Suppressed, because the officers did not get a valid consent.

---

a. Admitted, because the officers had probable cause to search the suitcase.
INCORRECT: Probable cause alone is never enough to conduct a search. Officers must, in addition, have a warrant, consent, or an exigent circumstance.

b. Admitted, because Marsh abandoned the suitcase.
CORRECT: By denying the suitcase was his, Marsh abandoned any REP he had in the suitcase and therefore, there was no 4th Amendment intrusion.

c. Suppressed, because the officers violated Marsh's reasonable expectation of privacy.
INCORRECT: A dog sniff of a suitcase in a public place is not a violation of REP. In addition, any REP marsh had he abandoned when he denied the suitcase was his.

d. Suppressed, because the officers did not get a valid consent.
INCORRECT: Consent was not necessary. Marsh abandoned his REP.

6. Perry is a paid police informant and has provided reliable information to officers on seven out of seven occasions. On January 7, 2000, Perry personally witnessed four personal-use drug transactions take place in Joe Clark's apartment. On November 28, 2000, Perry tells the officer about these observations. The officer applies for a search warrant for drugs based solely on this information. The request for the search warrant should be -

a. Denied, because the officer did not corroborated the information provided by Perry.

b. Denied, because the information provided by Perry is inadequate to establish probable cause.

c. Granted, because the officer has demonstrated probable cause.

d. Granted, because Perry meets the standards of Aguilar.

---

a. Denied, because the officer did not corroborated the information provided by Perry.
INCORRECT: Corroboration would do no good under the facts. The information is stale because almost eleven months has passed since the drugs were seen in Clark's apartment and therefore there is no PC there are drugs there NOW.

b. Denied, because the information provided by Perry is inadequate to establish probable cause.
CORRECT: The information is stale because almost eleven months has passed since the drugs were seen in Clark's apartment and therefore there is no PC there are drugs there NOW.

c. Granted, because the officer has demonstrated probable cause.
INCORRECT: There is no probable cause because the information is stale. Almost eleven months has passed since the drugs were seen in Clark's apartment and therefore there is no PC there are drugs there NOW.

d. Granted, because Perry meets the standards of Aguilar.
INCORRECT: The information is stale because almost eleven months has passed since the drugs were seen in Clark's apartment and therefore there is no PC there are drugs there NOW.

7. Police approach the home of Adams, whom they reasonably suspect is involved in a larceny. Adams is not there, but his wife is home. The officers explain they are looking for Adams and would like to talk to him about his clothing he was wearing the day before. Adams' wife states, "Those things are right here. I took them out of his duffel bag. Here they are" and hands them to the officer. The officers accepted the items. At trial, this evidence should be -

a. Suppressed, as they were obtained illegally without either a warrant or an exception to the warrant requirement.

b. Suppressed, because the officers had no probable cause to seek the items.

c. Admitted, because the officers could have gotten a search warrant to obtain these items.

d. Admitted, as the items were procured through private action, and thus, were not a search under the 4th Amendment.

---

a. Suppressed, as they were obtained illegally without either a warrant or an exception to the warrant requirement.
INCORRECT: This was a private search and therefore, the 4th Amendment was not violated.

b. Suppressed, because the officers had no probable cause to seek the items.
INCORRECT: This was a private search and therefore, the 4th Amendment was not implicated.

c. Admitted, because the officers could have gotten a search warrant to obtain these items.
INCORRECT: PC, not RS, is required to obtain a search warrant.

d. Admitted, as the items were procured through private action, and thus, were not a search under the 4th Amendment.
CORRECT: This answer correctly states the applicable principle.

8. Two officers develop reasonable suspicion that Smith is about to rob a convenience store. The officers approach Smith, place him under arrest, and search him. The officer conducting the search feels what is immediately apparent to him to be crack cocaine. The officer then retrieved the substance. At trial, Smith makes a motion to suppress the crack cocaine found during the search. According to the law, this motion should be:

a. Denied, based on the "plain touch" doctrine.

b. Denied, because the officers were justified in conducting a search on Smith.

c. Granted, because the officers acted illegally.

d. Granted, because an officer may lawfully retrieve only weapons during a frisk.

---

a. Denied, based on the "plain touch" doctrine.
INCORRECT: The officers arrested Smith when they only had R/S. PC is required to arrest and therefore the search of Smith was illegal.

b. Denied, because the officers were justified in conducting a search on Smith.
INCORRECT: The officers arrested Smith when they only had R/S. PC is required to arrest and therefore the search of Smith was illegal.

c. Granted, because the officers acted illegally.
CORRECT: The officers arrested Smith when they only had R/S. PC is required to arrest and therefore the search of Smith was illegal.

d. Granted, because an officer may lawfully retrieve only weapons during a frisk.
INCORRECT: During a terry frisk, officers may retrieve weapons, hard objects that could be a weapon, and anything that is immediately apparent to be contraband under the plain touch doctrine.

9. An officer receives a report from the dispatcher about an armed robbery in the area, along with a description of the vehicle and the three men believed to have committed the crime. Spotting a vehicle matching the description, with three male occupants inside, the officer stops the vehicle to investigate. She directs the three occupants from the vehicle, and examines the vehicle for weapons. Under the front passenger seat, the officer finds a sawed-off shotgun and some ski masks. All three men are then arrested. At trial, the men file a motion to suppress the evidence found in the vehicle. According to the law, this motion should be:

a. Granted, because the officer did not frisk the occupants of the vehicle prior to frisking the actual vehicle.

b. Granted, because the officer did not have reasonable suspicion to frisk the interior of the vehicle.

c. Denied, because the officer had obtained valid consent to search the interior of the vehicle.

d. Denied, because the officer was justified in looking under the front passenger seat for weapons.

---

a. Granted, because the officer did not frisk the occupants of the vehicle prior to frisking the actual vehicle.
INCORRECT: There is no requirement to frisk the occupants before frisking the car.

b. Granted, because the officer did not have reasonable suspicion to frisk the interior of the vehicle.
INCORRECT: The report, the description, and the fact the vehicle and occupants generally matching the description is RS criminal activity is afoot. Because the crime under suspicion is one in which a weapon is often used, there is also RS the occupants are presently armed and dangerous. This permits a Terry frisk of the occupants and under the seat (as well as the passenger compartment and unlocked containers therein) for weapons.

c. Denied, because the officer had obtained valid consent to search the interior of the vehicle.
INCORRECT: There are no facts to suggest the occupants consented to the frisk of the car.

d. Denied, because the officer was justified in looking under the front passenger seat for weapons.
CORRECT: The report, the description, and the fact the vehicle and occupants generally matching the description is RS criminal activity is afoot. Because the crime under suspicion is one in which a weapon is often used, there is also RS the occupants are presently armed and dangerous. This permits a Terry frisk of the occupants and under the seat (as well as the passenger compartment and unlocked containers therein) for weapons.

10. Jones is a Park Ranger with the National Park Service. He sees Smith driving inside a national park. Based on reasonable suspicion that Smith has committed a federal felony (larceny), Jones gives chase and pulls Smith over. Jones directs Smith out of his car and after repeating the direction several times, Smith complies. Smith then is belligerent and argumentative, wanders about, keeps turning his side to Officer Jones and repeatedly reaches into the pocket that Jones can't see even after being told to keep still and keep his hands out of his pocket. Jones then places Smith into handcuffs, frisks him, places Smith into the rear of the police car, and frisks the passenger compartment and trunk for weapons. In the trunk Jones finds drugs in plain view that are offered against Smith at trial. Will the drugs be admissible at trial?

a. Yes, because Smith's actions permitted a frisk of the trunk.

b. Yes, because Smith may search a mobile conveyance without PC or a warrant.

c. No, because ordering Smith out of the car and handcuffing him was a 4th Amendment violation making the search also illegal.

d. No, because Jones could not frisk the trunk under the facts provided.

---

a. Yes, because Smith's actions permitted a frisk of the trunk.
INCORRECT: Jones could frisk the passenger compartment for weapons because he had RS that Smith was presently armed and dangerous. To go into the trunk, however, Jones needed consent or PC. (The mobile conveyance exception would excuse having to obtain a warrant.)

b. Yes, because Smith may search a mobile conveyance without either PC or a warrant.
INCORRECT: Smith may search a mobile conveyance without a warrant, but PC is still required.

c. No, because ordering Smith out of the car and handcuffing him was a 4th Amendment violation making the search also illegal.
INCORRECT: An officer may direct a driver from his car during a Terry stop. Reasonable force, to include handcuffs, may be used under this circumstances because of Smith's non-compliance, walking about, and making furtive gestures after being told not to.

d. No, because Jones could not frisk the trunk under the facts provided.
CORRECT: A frisk of Jones for weapons is permissible because there is RS he is presently armed and dangerous based upon his belligerence, movements, non-compliance, and the way he kept reaching into his pockets and turning away. The vehicle can also be frisked but the trunk cannot. Also, Jones had only RS and there are no facts that give him PC to go into the trunk.

11. Two federal officers develop reasonable suspicion that Smith is about to rob the Federal Credit Union. The officers approach Smith, identify themselves as federal officers, and instruct him to place his hands on the wall. One of the officers conducts a frisk of Smith, and, upon touching Smith's right front pants pocket, discovers what is immediately apparent to him to be crack cocaine. The officer retrieves the cocaine and arrests Smith. At his trial for possession of narcotics, Smith files a motion to suppress all evidence obtained during the frisk. According to the law, this evidence will be:

a. Admissible, because the officer discovered the cocaine through the "plain touch" doctrine.

b. Admissible, because a frisk for evidence, including narcotics, may always be conducted following a valid Terry stop.

c. Suppressed, because a Terry frisk may only be utilized to discover readily accessible weapons that a suspect may use against an officer during an investigatory stop.

d. Suppressed, because the officer could not lawfully conduct a frisk of Smith.

---

a. Admissible, because the officer discovered the cocaine through the "plain touch" doctrine.
CORRECT: Three elements must be present before the "plain touch" doctrine will permit evidence to be seized during a Terry frisk: First, the frisk itself must be lawful; second, the incriminating nature of the item must be immediately apparent to the officer; and third, the discovery is limited to the initial touching, without further manipulation. All three elements are present in this scenario.

b. Admissible, because a frisk for evidence, including narcotics, may always be conducted following a valid Terry stop.
INCORRECT: A frisk may not always be permissible following a Terry stop. In order to lawfully frisk a suspect, an officer must have reasonable suspicion to believe that the suspect is presently armed and dangerous. If this suspicion exists, the officer may do a protective pat-down of the suspect looking for any weapons that might be utilized against the officer during the investigatory stop. An officer may not, however, conduct a Terry frisk to discover evidence of a crime.

c. Suppressed, because a Terry frisk may only be utilized to discover readily accessible weapons that a suspect may use against an officer during an investigatory stop.
INCORRECT: While a law enforcement officer may not frisk a suspect looking for evidence of a crime, where immediately incriminating evidence is uncovered during a lawful Terry frisk, the law does not require that an officer turn a blind eye to it. In such circumstances, the officer may seize the incriminating evidence, even though the evidence is not a weapon.

d. Suppressed, because the officer could not lawfully conduct a frisk of Smith.
INCORRECT: The officers had reasonable suspicion that Smith was about to commit a robbery. Because of the nature of this offense, the officers had reasonable suspicion to believe that Smith was presently armed and dangerous. With this level of suspicion, the officers were entitled to conduct the frisk for weapons.

12. Brown is suspected of being involved in a conspiracy to traffic narcotics. Agents learn that Brown has a houseboat docked at a lake 147 miles from his home. While Brown has not been on the boat for more than two years, he has kept up the mooring fees and registration of the vessel. The agents reasonably suspect that evidence of the narcotics conspiracy will be found on the boat. Once the boat is located, three agents board the boat to conduct a search. While no evidence of narcotics trafficking is found, the agents do find evidence of an unrelated murder in the cabin. At his trial for murder, Brown makes a pretrial motion to suppress the evidence found on the boat. According to the law, this evidence will be:

a. Admissible, because the warrantless search of a mobile conveyance is an exception to the warrant requirement of the Fourth Amendment.

b. Admissible, because Brown has, through his actions, given up any reasonable expectation of privacy in the boat.

c. Inadmissible, because the mobile conveyance exception to the warrant requirement does not apply in this case.

d. Inadmissible, because the agents primary motive in searching the boat was to discover evidence of narcotics trafficking.

---

a. Admissible, because the warrantless search of a mobile conveyance is an exception to the warrant requirement of the Fourth Amendment.
INCORRECT: While the warrantless search of a mobile conveyance (i.e., a Carroll search) is an exception to the Fourth Amendment, the requirements for that type of search are not present in this case. A Carroll search requires probable cause, rather than reasonable suspicion. If probable cause does not exist, a Carroll search is impermissible.

b. Admissible, because Brown has, through his actions, given up any reasonable expectation of privacy in the boat.
INCORRECT: While Brown has not been on the boat for more than two years, it is clear that he has not abandoned the boat, nor his expectation of privacy in it. By keeping up the mooring and registration fees, Brown is retaining his privacy interest in the boat.

c. Inadmissible, because the mobile conveyance exception to the warrant requirement does not apply in this case.
CORRECT: The mobile conveyance exception to the warrant requirement does not apply in this case because probable cause is not present. The mobile conveyance exception requires both probable cause and ready mobility before a warrantless search can be conducted.

d. Inadmissible, because the agents primary motive in searching the boat was to discover evidence of narcotics trafficking.
INCORRECT: The agents' primary motive in searching the boat is irrelevant to the evidence that was ultimately discovered. Had the agents been lawfully on the boat, any evidence of another crime that was discovered could have been admissible under the "plain view" doctrine.

13. A federal agent is having dinner in a restaurant located in a federal park (an area of exclusive jurisdiction), when the manager, whom the agent knows, approaches him. The manager states that two young men have just left the restaurant without paying for their dinners (a federal misdemeanor), and asks the agent to arrest them before they can escape. The agent quickly leaves the restaurant and, based upon a detailed physical description given by the manager, is able to locate the two suspects walking down the sidewalk approximately two blocks from the restaurant. To arrest the suspects, an arrest warrant is:

a. required, because the offense did not occur in the agent's presence.

b. required, because a misdemeanor arrest may never be made in a public place without first obtaining an arrest warrant.

c. not required, because based on the statements from the manager of the restaurant, the agent had probable cause to make the arrest.

d. not required, because a misdemeanor arrest may always be made in a public place without first obtaining an arrest warrant.

---

a. required, because the offense did not occur in the agent's presence.
CORRECT: Under federal law, warrantless misdemeanor arrests may be made in a public place if the crime was committed in the presence of the arresting officer. If the crime was not committed in the presence of the arresting officer, an arrest warrant must be obtained.

b. required, because a misdemeanor arrest may never be made in a public place without first obtaining an arrest warrant.
INCORRECT: Under federal law, warrantless misdemeanor arrests may be made in a public place if the crime was committed in the presence of the arresting officer. If the crime was not committed in the presence of the arresting officer, an arrest warrant must be obtained.

c. not required, because based on the statements from the manager of the restaurant, the agent had probable cause to make the arrest.
INCORRECT: For a warrantless misdemeanor arrest in a public place, in addition to the probable cause requirement, it is also necessary that the offense occur in the law enforcement officer's presence (i.e., within sight or other senses).

d. not required, because a misdemeanor arrest may always be made in a public place without first obtaining an arrest warrant.
INCORRECT: Under federal law, warrantless misdemeanor arrests may be made in a public place if the crime was committed in the presence of the arresting officer.

14. Federal agents are investigating Davis for wire and mail fraud. They arrange to interview Davis at his home about the allegations. During the course of the interview, the agents ask Davis if they could search his home office for various documents. When Davis stayed silent, one of the agents responds, "Listen, if you say no, we're going to apply for a search warrant, and, if we get it, we're going to come back and search then." Davis then tells the agents they can search his home office. During the course of the search, documents are discovered linking Davis to the wire and mail fraud allegations. At his trial on these charges, Davis makes a motion to suppress the evidence found during the search of his office, claiming that his consent was not voluntarily given. According to the law, this motion will be:

a. Granted, because Davis' consent was not voluntarily given, but was mere submission to the authority of the law enforcement agents.

b. Granted, because the agents did not notify Davis that he had the right to refuse to grant consent for the search.

c. Denied, because the agent's statement regarding his intent to apply for a search warrant was permissible.

d. Denied, because when David stayed silent, probable cause arose to conduct the search either with or without a search warrant.

---

a. Granted, because Davis' consent was not voluntarily given, but was mere submission to the authority of the law enforcement agents.
INCORRECT: Submission by the individual to the authority of the law enforcement officer does not constitute consent. Consent is not voluntarily given in response to an officer's statement that the officer has come to search with a warrant when, in fact, there is none, or they will get a warrant if consent is withheld. However, it is permissible for officers truthfully to advise a person that they will apply for a warrant if consent is refused.

b. Granted, because the agents did not notify Davis that he had the right to refuse to grant consent for the search.
INCORRECT: Whether consent is freely and voluntarily given is decided by the facts as decided by the court, which will consider all of the surrounding circumstances. One of these circumstances is knowledge of the right to withhold consent, though such knowledge is not essential. An officer is not required to advise a person of their right to refuse consent.

c. Denied, because the agent's statement regarding his intent to apply for a search warrant was permissible.
CORRECT: Submission by the individual to the authority of the law enforcement officer does not constitute consent. Consent is not voluntarily given in response to an officer's statement that the officer has come to search with a warrant when, in fact, there is none, or they will get a warrant if consent is withheld. However, it is permissible for officers truthfully to advise a person that they will apply for a warrant if consent is refused.

d. Denied, because when David stayed silent, probable cause arose to conduct the search either with or without a search warrant.
INCORRECT: Davis' silence cannot be used to establish probable cause for the search. Additionally, even if it could, probable cause, standing alone, is never enough for a search. Instead, the agents would need to justify a warrantless search with an exception to the warrant requirement. Based on the facts presented, no such exception exists in this case.

15. A law enforcement officer has a hunch that Roberts is trafficking narcotics. After observing Roberts speed through a stop sign, the law enforcement officer decided to pull Roberts over for the traffic violation, so that he could try to discover evidence of narcotics in the vehicle. The officer turned on his overhead lights and performed a traffic stop. Once Roberts' car stopped, the officer approached the car and instructed Roberts to roll down his window. As Roberts did so, the officer was faced with the overwhelming odor of raw marijuana emanating from the car. The officer requested Robert's identification and registration, and Roberts complied. After checking the identification through dispatch, the officer wrote out a citation, had Roberts sign it, and returned the identification and registration documents to Roberts. Before Roberts could leave, however, the officer ordered him to step out of the vehicle. Roberts complied, and the officer began to search various areas within the car. In the trunk of the vehicle, under the spare wheel, the officer discovered what later turned out to be 10 kilos of marijuana. At his trial, Roberts filed a motion to suppress the evidence because of an illegal search of the vehicle. According to the law, this motion will be:

a. Granted, because, while the officer could detain Roberts as long as reasonably necessary to check his identification and issue a warning or citation to him, once those purposes were accomplished, the officer was required to let Roberts go.

b. Granted, because the officer's initial traffic was simply a pretext used to investigate for narcotics.

c. Denied, because the officer had the ability to perform a Terry frisk for weapons that could have been located in the vehicle.

d. Denied, because the marijuana was found during a valid search of the vehicle's trunk.

---

a. Granted, because, while the officer could detain Roberts as long as reasonably necessary to check his identification and issue a warning or citation to him, once those purposes were accomplished, the officer was required to let Roberts go.
INCORRECT: An officer may detain the driver of a vehicle as long as reasonably necessary to request the driver's license and registration; request the driver to step out of the vehicle; conduct computer inquiries to determine the validity of the license and registration; conduct computer searches to investigate the driver's criminal history and to determine if the driver has outstanding warrant; and issue a warning or citation. However, once the initial reason for the stop has been accomplished, the stop must end, unless something occurs during the traffic stop that generates reasonable suspicion to justify a further detention. The smell of raw marijuana in this case provided the justification for the additional detention of Roberts.

b. Granted, because the officer's initial traffic was simply a pretext used to investigate for narcotics.
INCORRECT: Pretextual traffic stops have been found to be permissible, so long as either reasonable suspicion or probable cause existed for the initial stop. In this case, the traffic infraction allowed the officer to stop Roberts, so the pretextual nature of the stop is irrelevant.

c. Denied, because the officer had the ability to perform a Terry frisk for weapons that could have been located in the vehicle.
INCORRECT: Even conceding that the officers could perform a Terry frisk in this scenario, such a frisk would not have permissibly included the trunk of the vehicle, in that any weapons located in that area would not be readily accessible to the suspect.

d. Denied, because the marijuana was found during a valid search of the vehicle's trunk.
CORRECT: The odor of raw marijuana emanating from the vehicle gave the officer probable cause to search the vehicle without a warrant pursuant to the Carroll doctrine. When performing a Carroll search, an officer may look anywhere within the vehicle where what he is seeking could be hidden, which in this case includes the trunk.

4th Amendment Practice Exam

16. Federal agents suspect that Martin is dealing in narcotics from his home, a felony offense, but have not been able to obtain enough evidence to justify issuance of a search or arrest warrant. They take up surveillance from various positions around the neighborhood, while an undercover officer approaches the residence in an attempt to buy narcotics. As the agents observe, the undercover officer approaches Martin, who is sitting on his front porch, and engages in a lengthy discussion. When an object is transferred between Martin and the undercover officer, the officer gives the signal that narcotics have been exchanged. The agents, dressed in raid jackets and marked vehicles, descend on the house to arrest Martin for narcotics distribution. As Martin sees the agents approach, he turns, runs directly into his home, and slams the door behind him. One of the agents breaks through the door, and is able to catch Martin as he is trying to run through the kitchen. Martin has a bag of what appears to be cocaine in his hand when he is arrested, and various other drugs are found on a table next to where the arrest occurred. Did the officers violate 18 U.S.C. § 3109 (the Federal "knock and announce" statute)?

a. No, because an agent may always make a warrantless entry into a residence to make an arrest, so long as probable cause exists.

b. No, because the agents entered the house to make the arrest under exigent circumstances.

c. Yes, because the agents did not announce their identity and purpose.

d. Yes, because the statute must always be complied with whenever an officer desires to enter a private residence.

---

a. No, because an agent may always make a warrantless entry into a residence to make an arrest, so long as probable cause exists.
INCORRECT: An agent may not make a warrantless entry into a residence to make an arrest for any offense; the offense must be a felony (Welsh v. Wisconsin).

b. No, because the agents entered the house to make the arrest under exigent circumstances.
CORRECT: Based on the signal provided by the undercover officer, the agents had probable cause to make the arrest. When Martin turned and ran into the residence, the officers were in "hot pursuit." They had probable cause to arrest for a felony, and a general and continuous knowledge (within reason) of the suspect's whereabouts.

c. Yes, because the agents did not announce their identity and purpose.
INCORRECT: Agents who are in "hot pursuit" need not comply with Title 18 U.S.C. § 3109.

d. Yes, because officers must always comply with the statute whenever an officer desires to enter a private residence.
INCORRECT: This statement is far too broad to be close to being correct. (1). The statute provides only that the officers cannot break to enter to execute a search or arrest warrant unless the officer first identifies his authority and purpose. An officer could then enter with consent of the occupant without complying with the statute. (2). Exigent circumstances will excuse compliance with the statute. See also the justification for answer b.

17. Two federal agents have been investigating Thomas and have reasonable suspicion to believe that he is selling false identification documents out of the trunk of his vehicle. Upon seeing him parked in a public parking lot, they approach him, identify themselves as federal agents, and ask him to place his hands on top of the vehicle. During the frisk that follows, one of the officers feels what he reasonably believes is a handgun. He retrieves the item and confirms that the object is a .22 caliber pistol. Knowing that Thomas was previously convicted of a felony (theft), the agent places him under arrest for being a felon-in-possession. A search of the vehicle incident to the arrest turns up a bag of false identification documents under the back seat of Thomas' vehicle. At his trial on weapons and false identification documents, Thomas makes a motion to suppress all of the evidence recovered by the agents. According to the law:

a. The pistol will be admitted, but the false identification documents will be suppressed.

b. The pistol will be suppressed, but the false identification documents will be admitted.

c. All of the evidence will be admitted.

d. None of the evidence will be admitted.

---

a. The pistol will be admitted, but the false identification documents will be suppressed.
INCORRECT: All of the evidence would be suppressed. The agents had reasonable suspicion to temporarily detain Thomas for investigation. However, they did not have the right to conduct a frisk on him, in that the offense being investigated is not generally associated with being "armed and dangerous." Because the frisk was impermissible (i.e., the agents did not have reasonable suspicion that Thomas was presently armed and dangerous), the pistol discovered during the frisk would be suppressed. The false identifications would be suppressed as the fruit of an illegal search (i.e., the fruit of an invalid search incident to arrest). Note that even if an SIA was permissible, the scope of a vehicle SIA does not include the trunk.

b. The pistol will be suppressed, but the false identification documents will be admitted.
INCORRECT: See justification a.

c. All of the evidence will be admitted.
INCORRECT: See justification a.

d. None of the evidence will be admitted.
CORRECT: See justification a.

18. Federal agents have an arrest warrant for Moore for failure to appear. At approximately 12:00 a.m. one night, the agents approach Moore's home, reasonably believing that he is inside. As they open the unlocked door and enter, all of the agents clearly announce, "Federal agents!" Immediately inside the door, Moore is found sitting on a sofa in the living room. On coffee table in front of him, the agents see a white powdery substance (later determined to be cocaine), scales, small baggies, and other pieces of drug paraphernalia. Moore is arrested, and is charged with possession of cocaine and drug paraphernalia. Which of the following statements is correct?

a. Title 18 U.S.C. § 3109 was NOT violated because it applies only to the execution of search warrants, not arrest warrants.

b. Title 18 U.S.C. § 3109 was NOT violated because entering through an unlocked door does not qualify as "break[ing] open any outer or inner door" of a house, as required by Title 18 U.S.C. § 3109.

c. The agents executed the warrant outside of the time limit prescribed by statute, specifically, between 6:00 a.m. and 10:00 p.m.

d. The agents were required to comply with Title 18 U.S.C. § 3109 (knock and announce) and failed to do so.

---

a. Title 18 U.S.C. § 3109 was NOT violated because it applies only to the execution of search warrants, not arrest warrants.
INCORRECT: Title 18 U.S.C. § 3109 has been held to apply to all entries under color of law, either to search or to arrest, with or without a warrant. While the statute speaks exclusively of search warrants, case law has interpreted the statute to include entries for the execution of arrest warrants.

b. Title 18 U.S.C. § 3109 was NOT violated because entering through an unlocked door does not qualify as "break[ing] open any outer or inner door" of a house, as required by Title 18 U.S.C. § 3109.
INCORRECT: The courts have given a broad construction to this statute. For instance, the word "break" has been interpreted to include opening an unlocked door or using a passkey. In this instance, the entry clearly constituted a "breaking" by the agent, even though the door to the home was unlocked.

c. The agents executed the warrant outside of the time limit prescribed by statute, specifically, between 6:00 a.m. and 10:00 p.m.
INCORRECT: Unlike a federal search warrant, a federal arrest warrant may be executed by any authorized officer at any time within the jurisdiction of the United States, its possessions, and its territories. Pursuant to Rule 41(h) of the Federal Rules of Criminal Procedure, a federal search warrant must normally be served in the daytime, which is defined as the hours between 6:00 a.m. to 10:00 p.m.

d. The agents were required to comply with Title 18 U.S.C. § 3109 (knock and announce) and failed to do so.
CORRECT: The agents in this case failed to comply with Title 18 U.S.C. § 3109. Specifically, the agents failed to announce their authority and purpose. Merely stating "Federal agents" is insufficient. The agents must also state their purpose (e.g., "Federal agents with a search warrant"). Additionally, the agents in this case impermissibly used force to enter prior to being refused admittance. The term "refused admittance" means that an agent must wait a reasonable length of time before forcing entry, unless exigent circumstances exist.

19. Federal agents develop probable cause that Gibson's garage contains a large quantity of counterfeit social security checks. They also have reason to suspect that, earlier in the morning, their confidential informant told Gibson that they were about to apply for a search warrant, and that Gibson indicated he would destroy the evidence after he returns home from an out-of-town visit. The agents approach Gibson's home and are certain he has not yet arrived and no one is at home. After discussing their options, the agents force their way through the garage door and into the home. During the subsequent search, they seize hundreds of counterfeit social security checks. Approximately ninety minutes later, Gibson returns home and is placed under arrest. At his trial, he makes a motion to suppress the evidence discovered during the warrantless search of his home. According to the law, this evidence will be:

a. Admitted, because the agents would have inevitably discovered the evidence once they applied for a search warrant.

b. Admitted, because the agents entered the home due to exigent circumstances (destruction of evidence).

c. Suppressed, because the agents did not have probable cause to arrest Gibson at the time of the search.

d. Suppressed, because the agents had time to apply for a telephonic warrant.

---

a. Admitted, because the agents would have inevitably discovered the evidence once they applied for a search warrant.
INCORRECT: The "inevitable discovery" doctrine means that the unreasonable search or seizure of evidence by one officer will not bar the use of that evidence when other officers, acting independently and without knowledge of the wrongful acts of the first officer, are searching lawfully for the evidence. Since no independent search was being conducted at the time of the illegal search in this case, the "inevitable discovery" doctrine does not apply.

b. Admitted, because the agents entered the home due to exigent circumstances (destruction of evidence).
INCORRECT: An exigent circumstances will justify a warrantless search when law enforcement officers reasonably believe that the removal or destruction of evidence is imminent, and there is not enough time to secure a search warrant. In this case, the removal or destruction of the evidence was not imminent, because the suspect was not home at the time.

c. Suppressed, because the agents did not have probable cause to arrest Gibson at the time of the search.
INCORRECT: The issue of probable cause to arrest Gibson is irrelevant to determining whether the warrantless search of the house in this scenario was reasonable under the Fourth Amendment.

d. Suppressed, because the agents had time to apply for a telephonic warrant.
CORRECT: Occasionally, law enforcement officers are confronted with a situation in which they do not have time to obtain a warrant in the traditional manner due to the impending destruction or removal of evidence. Rule 41(c)(2) of the Federal Rules of Criminal Procedure provides for a search warrant based on oral testimony, such as communicated by telephone or facsimile machine. This procedure may drastically reduce the time it takes to obtain a search warrant. Thus, if law enforcement officers have time to attempt to secure a telephonic search warrant before the removal or destruction becomes imminent, the officers should attempt to do so. Failure to attempt to secure a telephonic search warrant, if the opportunity was available, may be considered in an unfavorable manner by a reviewing court.

20. Federal agents obtain a valid premises search warrant to look for pornographic materials in Black's home. When the warrant is executed, the agents properly knock, announce their identity and purpose, and demand admittance. Black opens the door and the agents enter. Immediately, the agents notice that four other people are inside the house. One of the individuals is recognized as Black's live-in girlfriend, Courtney. The other three persons are unknown. Without hesitating, the agents order all five people to stand and face the wall, where a frisk is conducted for the safety of the officers. During the frisk of Courtney, one agent discovers what is immediately apparent to him to be crack cocaine. He reaches in, retrieves the item, and confirms that it is cocaine. Courtney is arrested. At her trial for narcotics possession, Courtney makes a motion to suppress the cocaine. According to the law, this motion will be:

a. Granted, because, pursuant to the premises search warrant, the agents could not conduct a frisk of Courtney.

b. Granted, because, pursuant to the premises search warrant, the agents could only frisk Black, the owner of the property.

c. Denied, because the agents had a valid search warrant for the premises, and were allowed to search any occupants of the premises pursuant to that warrant.

d. Denied, because the agents had a valid search warrant for the premises, and were allowed to frisk any occupants of the premises pursuant to that warrant.

---

a. Granted, because, pursuant to the premises search warrant, the agents could not conduct a frisk of Courtney.
CORRECT: A premises search warrant does not allow law enforcement officers to either frisk or search persons who may be present on the premises at the time the warrant is executed. Instead, to frisk any individual present during the execution of a premises search warrant, agents need reasonable suspicion to believe that the individual is presently armed and dangerous. There are no facts present to support the belief that the persons in this scenario were either armed or dangerous.

b. Granted, because, pursuant to the premises search warrant, the agents could only frisk Black, the owner of the property.
INCORRECT: A premises search warrant does not allow law enforcement officers to either frisk or search persons who may be present on the premises at the time the warrant is executed.

c. Denied, because the agents had a valid search warrant for the premises, and were allowed to search any occupants of the premises pursuant to that warrant.
INCORRECT: A premises search warrant does not allow law enforcement officers to either frisk or search persons who may be present on the premises at the time the warrant is executed.

d. Denied, because the agents had a valid search warrant for the premises, and were allowed to frisk any occupants of the premises pursuant to that warrant.
INCORRECT: A premises search warrant does not allow law enforcement officers to either frisk or search persons who may be present on the premises at the time the warrant is executed. Instead, to frisk any individual present during the execution of a premises search warrant, agents need reasonable suspicion to believe that the individual is presently armed and dangerous. There are no facts present to support the belief that the persons in this scenario were either armed or dangerous.

21. An undercover officer purchased controlled substances from King yesterday and today a warrant was issued for King's arrest. Officers spotted King in his usual place in a high crime area where he had been seen selling drugs the day before from his car. King was arrested on the warrant. After arresting King and placing him in handcuffs, the officer had him sit in the back of the officer's vehicle. The officer then returned to King's vehicle and began to search it. Under the front passenger seat, the officer found a bag containing cocaine. Under the back seat, the officer found rolling papers. The officer then opened the trunk of the vehicle and began to search it. Immediately, 6 bricks of marijuana were discovered. At his trial for possession of controlled substances, King makes a motion to suppress all of the evidence found in his vehicle. According to the law:

a. The cocaine and rolling papers will be admitted, while the 6 bricks of marijuana will be suppressed.

b. The cocaine and rolling papers will be suppressed, while the 6 bricks of marijuana will be admitted.

c. All of the evidence is admissible.

d. None of the evidence is admissible.

---

a. The cocaine and rolling papers will be admitted, while the 6 bricks of marijuana will be suppressed.
INCORRECT: The cocaine and rolling papers are admissible because they were lawfully found during a valid search incident to arrest of the passenger compartment of the vehicle. Based on the recent warrant, the nature of the offenses, and activities observed on the day of arrest, the officers had reasonable to believe that evidence of the crime of arrest (drug sale) was in the vehicle. The bricks of marijuana are also admissible, not because they were found during a valid search incident to arrest of the vehicle, but under the mobile conveyance exception. The discoveries in the passenger compartment established probable cause to search the trunk of the vehicle.

b. The cocaine and rolling papers will be suppressed, while the 6 bricks of marijuana will be admitted.
INCORRECT: See justification a.

c. All of the evidence is admissible.
CORRECT: See justification a.

d. None of the evidence is admissible.
INCORRECT: See justification a.

22. Law enforcement officers receive notice from their dispatcher that there has been a homicide at a local apartment building. Arriving at the designated apartment, the officers notice that the door to the apartment has what appear to be bullet holes in it, and that the lock on the door is broken. Without first obtaining a search warrant, the officers push open the door and enter the apartment. Inside, they find a deceased male and a female who is unconscious, but appears to have suffered a self-inflicted gunshot wound to the chest. Emergency personnel are called, and both bodies are removed from the scene of the crime. After securing the apartment, two of the officers begin to process the crime scene looking for evidence. In a trashcan near the kitchen, the officers find a crumpled note. Not sure if it's evidence or not, the officers read the note and discover it was written by the woman. The note indicates that she had killed the man (her husband) because of an illicit affair he was having, and that she was going to kill herself. The woman recovers and is charged with her husband's murder. At her trial, she makes a motion to suppress the note found in the trashcan. According to the law, this evidence will be:

a. Admitted, because the officers entered the apartment and conducted the warrantless search pursuant to the emergency scene exception to the Fourth Amendment's warrant requirement.

b. Admitted, because the note was found in plain view during the processing of the homicide scene.

c. Suppressed, because the officers were not authorized to enter the apartment without first obtaining a search warrant.

d. Suppressed, because the search by the officers was made without either a search warrant or an exception to the Fourth Amendment's warrant requirement.

---

a. Admitted, because the officers entered the apartment and conducted the warrantless search pursuant to the emergency scene exception to the Fourth Amendment's warrant requirement.
INCORRECT: While the initial entry into the apartment was justified under the "emergency scene" exception to the warrant requirement, once the exigency ended (i.e., once the bodies were removed from the scene) the officers' legal justification for being in the apartment terminated. To process this crime scene after that point, the officers needed to secure a search warrant.

b. Admitted, because the note was found in plain view during the processing of the homicide scene.
INCORRECT: The note was not found in plain view. First, at the time the note was discovered, the officers were not lawfully on the premises. Second, the incriminating nature of the note was not immediately apparent at the time it was seized by the officers.

c. Suppressed, because the officers were not authorized to enter the apartment without first obtaining a search warrant.
INCORRECT: The officers were entitled to enter the apartment because of the emergency nature of the dispatch call. In these instances, officers do not have time to obtain a search warrant to justify their entry. This type of "exigent" circumstance is one of the few established exceptions to the Fourth Amendment's warrant requirement.

d. Suppressed, because the search by the officers was made without either a search warrant or an exception to the Fourth Amendment's warrant requirement.
CORRECT: At the time the note was found, the officers were no longer lawfully on the premises. The exigency that justified their warrantless entry no longer existed, because the victim and suspect had been removed from the scene. To continue to search at this point, the officers needed to obtain a warrant.

23. Armed with an arrest warrant for Jones for mail fraud and false statements, federal agents approach Jones' home. Surveillance has indicated that, in the previous 48 hours, no one other than Jones has entered or left the premises. The officers have no additional information that anyone other than Jones is located inside the two-story home. The agents knock on the door, announce their identity and purpose, and demand entry. When the agents hear footsteps running towards the rear of the residence, they use force to enter and make the arrest. Jones is arrested approximately ten feet from the back door of the residence. Two officers fan out to conduct a protective sweep of the home, and in the bathroom located on the second floor, discover marijuana shoved into the toilet tank. At his trial on possession charges, Jones files a motion to suppress the evidence found in the bathroom. According to the law, this motion will be:

a. Granted, because the agents had only an arrest warrant, and not a search warrant, they were not authorized to enter Jones' home.

b. Granted, because the marijuana was found during a search that violated the Fourth Amendment.

c. Denied, because the agents discovered the marijuana during a lawful protective sweep of the residence.

d. Denied, because the arrest warrant authorized the agents to conduct a search of the entire home incident to Jones' arrest.

---

a. Granted, because the agents had only an arrest warrant, and not a search warrant, they were not authorized to enter Jones' home.
INCORRECT: An arrest warrant carries with it the authority to enter a suspect's home in order to effect the arrest, so long as the agents reasonably believed that the suspect was in the home at the time the warrant was executed.

b. Granted, because the marijuana was found during a search that violated the Fourth Amendment.
CORRECT: There were two problems associated with the discovery of the marijuana in the scenario. First, an extended protective sweep requires reasonable suspicion to believe that an individual is in the home that could pose a danger to the agents. No facts exist in this question to justify the extended protective sweep in this case. Second, during a protective sweep, an agent may only look in those locations where a person could be hidden. In this case, looking into the toilet tank exceeded the lawful scope of a protective sweep.

c. Denied, because the agents discovered the marijuana during a lawful protective sweep of the residence.
INCORRECT: There were two problems associated with the discovery of the marijuana in the scenario. First, an extended protective sweep requires reasonable suspicion to believe that an individual is in the home that could pose a danger to the agents. No facts exist in this question to justify the extended protective sweep in this case. Second, during a protective sweep, an agent may only look in those locations where a person could be hidden. In this case, looking into the toilet tank exceeded the lawful scope of a protective sweep.

d. Denied, because the arrest warrant authorized the agents to conduct a search of the entire home incident to Jones' arrest.
INCORRECT: While an arrest warrant does authorize agents to enter a residence to effect an arrest (at least where they reasonably believe the suspect is inside the residence), it does not authorize them to search any further than is necessary to locate the suspect. In this case, once Jones was arrested, the immediate area of the arrest could be searched incident to the arrest. This does not include the upstairs bathroom.

24. Howard is arrested on a 6 year old warrant for income tax evasion as he is getting out of his car at his home. Howard has no other criminal history, and there is no reason to suspect that he has engaged in any other instance of income tax evasion or any other crime. As soon as he is handcuffed and his person searched, he is secured in the back of the patrol vehicle. Officers then search the passenger compartment of his car incident to arrest and find 10 ounces of marijuana in one ounce packages, scales, and baggies hidden in the glove compartment. The officers then decide to search the trunk of the car under the mobile conveyance exception and find 50 more ounces of marijuana hidden inside the spare tire. All the above evidence is seized and is offered as evidence at Howard's trial for possession with intent to distribute a controlled substance. Is the evidence admissible?

a. All the evidence is admissible.

b. None of the evidence is admissible.

c. The evidence found in the passenger compartment is admissible, but not the evidence in the trunk.

d. The evidence found in the trunk is admissible but not the evidence found in the passenger compartment because Howard was not an occupant of the vehicle at the time of the arrest.

---

a. All the evidence is admissible.
INCORRECT: See justification b.

b. None of the evidence is admissible.
CORRECT: The search incident to arrest of Howard's person was lawful and performed contemporaneous with the arrest. The officers could therefore search his person, and containers on his person, for weapons, means of escape, and any evidence of any crime. The search incident to arrest of the passenger compartment was not lawful. To search the passenger compartment of a vehicle when arresting an occupant or recent occupant, officers must be able to articulate that Howard still had access to the passenger compartment at the time of the search, and that was not the case as Howard was secured in the patrol vehicle. Officers could also perform a search incident to arrest of the passenger compartment if they had reason to believe that evidence of the crime of arrest was present. They had no such information. Had the search incident to arrest of the passenger compartment been lawful, the evidence found in the passenger compartment would have established probable cause there was evidence of crime in the trunk, and officers could have used the mobile conveyance exception to search there. Since the evidence found in the passenger compartment was unlawfully discovered, however, it cannot be used to establish probable cause for the mobile conveyance exception.

c. The evidence found in the passenger compartment is admissible, but not the evidence in the trunk.
INCORRECT: See justification b.

d. The evidence found in the trunk is admissible but not the evidence found in the passenger compartment because Howard was not an occupant of the vehicle at the time of the arrest.
INCORRECT: See justification b.

25. Morgan, a convicted felon, lived in a trailer owned by his girlfriend, Jones. Jones, anxious to defend herself against a charge, made by another woman, that she kept drugs at her home, invited two police officers to search the trailer. When the officers came in, Morgan was sitting in the living room. The officers explained to him that Jones had given consent for the search, and they then proceeded to make their search. In the bedroom shared by Jones and Morgan, the officers found a small bag with what appeared to be marijuana residue inside. Jones denied that the bag belonged to her, and told the officers that some of the items in the bedroom belonged to the defendant. On an upper shelf in the bedroom closet, in a jumble of boxes, tins, and bags belonging partly to Jones and partly to Morgan, the officers located a generic, unmarked tin box. In that box, they found what they believed to be a bomb made of dynamite, wires, and .9 mm. shells. During this time, Morgan remained in the living room and offered no objection to the search. Through questioning Jones, it was determined that the tin box belonged to Morgan, not her. Morgan was arrested and charged with being a felon in possession of explosives. At his trial, he made a motion to suppress the evidence found in the tin box. According to the law, the evidence will be:

a. Admitted, because Jones had apparent authority to consent to the search of the tin box.

b. Admitted, because Jones can consent to the search of any item within her residence, regardless of who the item actually belonged to.

c. Suppressed, because Jones did not have actual authority to consent to the search of the tin box.

d. Suppressed, because the officers exceeded the scope of the consent given them by Jones when they searched the tin box.

---

a. Admitted, because Jones had apparent authority to consent to the search of the tin box.
CORRECT: As the owner of the trailer, Jones freely gave consent to the search of the trailer, including the bedroom. The tin box was not identified in any way as belonging to Morgan, nor did Morgan attempt to limit Jones' consent to her own personal property. It was reasonable, then, for the officers to think that the tin box was within the consent that Jones had given. It was also reasonable for the officers to think that Jones had authority not only over the premises, but also over all of their contents not obviously belonging to someone else.

b. Admitted, because Jones can consent to the search of any item within her residence, regardless of who the item actually belonged to.
INCORRECT: For purposes of searches of closed containers, mere possession of the container by a third party does not necessarily give rise to a reasonable belief that the third party has authority to consent to a search of its contents. The key to consent is actual or apparent authority over the item to be searched. In deciding whether an individual has "apparent" authority over an item, courts consider various factors, including the nature of the container (e.g., was it a briefcase or a generic box?); whether there were external markings on the container, such as the defendant's name or the third party's name; and any precautions taken by the owner to ensure privacy, such as the use of locks or the government's knowledge of the defendant's orders not to open the container. With respect to locking mechanisms, courts also consider whether the defendant provided the third party with a combination or key to the lock.

c. Suppressed, because Jones did not have actual authority to consent to the search of the tin box.
INCORRECT: The probable cause and warrant requirements of the Fourth Amendment are not applicable where a party consents to a search, where a third party with common control over the searched premises consents, or where an individual with apparent authority to consent does so. As noted above, Jones had "apparent" authority to consent to the search, so "actual" authority is unnecessary.

d. Suppressed, because the officers exceeded the scope of the consent given them by Jones when they searched the tin box.
INCORRECT: Generally, consent to search a space includes consent to search containers within that space where a reasonable officer would construe the consent to extend to the container. As the owner of the trailer, Jones freely gave consent to the search of the trailer, including the bedroom. The tin box was not identified in any way as belonging to Morgan, nor did Morgan attempt to limit Jones' consent to her own personal property. It was reasonable, then, for the officers to think that the tin box was within the consent that Jones had given. It was also reasonable for the officers to think that Jones had authority not only over the premises, but also over all of their contents not obviously belonging to someone else.

26. After being issued a traffic citation, Morris decided to contest the ticket in court. On the day of his hearing, he approached the courthouse door and discovered that a magnetometer had been installed, with two security guards on either side of the device. As Morris got to the doorway, he was instructed by one of the guards that GSA regulations provided that anyone entering the courthouse would need to have their belongings searched and would need to step through the magnetometer. The purpose of these searches was to look for explosives or dangerous weapons. Morris refused to place his briefcase on the conveyor belt, stating that, because he had done nothing wrong, he did not feel it was proper to force him to endure this type of treatment. When notified that he would not be permitted to carry the briefcase into the courthouse without allowing the inspection, Morris grudgingly consented. When the briefcase was opened, one of the guards discovered a small bag containing marijuana in a side pocket. Was there a Fourth Amendment violation?

a. Yes, because the guards had no probable cause to believe that Morris had any explosives or dangerous weapons in his briefcase.

b. Yes, because the guards did not obtain a search warrant prior to searching Morris' briefcase for any explosives or dangerous weapons.

c. No, because the fact Morris was appearing at the courthouse gave the security guards reasonable suspicion to frisk his belongings prior to allowing him to enter.

d. No, because the search was validly conducted pursuant to GSA regulations and in compliance with the Fourth Amendment.

---

a. Yes, because the guards had no probable cause to believe that Morris had any explosives or dangerous weapons in his briefcase.
INCORRECT: Ordinarily, of course, a person should not have his person or property subjected to a search in the absence of a warrant or probable cause to believe that a crime is being committed. However, regulations that authorize warrantless inspections of persons and property entering federal courthouses comply with the Fourth Amendment. These searches are considered reasonable under the Fourth Amendment due to the balance that must be struck between the government's interest in safeguarding courthouses and the minimal intrusion that takes place during the inspection process.

b. Yes, because the guards did not obtain a search warrant prior to searching Morris' briefcase for any explosives or dangerous weapons.
INCORRECT: The key to any Fourth Amendment search, including an "administrative inspection," is reasonableness. To require that an officer obtain a warrant to examine the packages of each of the potentially hundreds of persons entering a federal facility or determine as to each person the existence of probable cause would, as a practical matter, seriously impair the power of government to protect itself against individuals who would commit destructive acts in or around courthouses.

c. No, because the fact Morris was appearing at the courthouse gave the security guards reasonable suspicion to frisk his belongings prior to allowing him to enter.
INCORRECT: Morris' appearance at the courthouse did not, in and of itself, give rise to reasonable suspicion to conduct a frisk of his belongings. Even assuming his appearance at a courthouse was sufficient justification to detain Morris, there is no evidence to support a reasonable suspicion he was presently armed and dangerous, the standard required for a Terry frisk.

d. No, because the search was validly conducted pursuant to GSA regulations and in compliance with the Fourth Amendment.
CORRECT: "Administrative inspections," though warrantless, are permissible under the 4th Amendment. A limited warrantless search of people (and their belongings) wishing to enter sensitive facilities is permitted if the search is part of a general practice (i.e., a regulation authorizing the inspection exists) and not for the purpose of securing evidence for criminal investigations. Both of those requirements are met in this case.

27. Based on their investigation, federal agents obtained a search warrant to search Smith's residence. The search warrant did not specifically list any vehicles to be searched, but rather authorized the search of the entire premises for methamphetamine. On the day the search was conducted, Smith's vehicle was parked in the driveway of his residence. During the course of the search, agents discovered numerous items of evidence, including a briefcase containing a vast quantity of methamphetamine. The agents then decided to search the vehicle, although they weren't sure any evidence was inside it. Inside the trunk of the vehicle, several kilos of cocaine were found. At his trial for drug trafficking, Smith made a motion to suppress the cocaine found in the vehicle's trunk. Did the agents violate the Fourth Amendment?

a. No, because it was found during the lawful execution of a premises search warrant.

b. No, because the vehicle was searched pursuant to the "mobile conveyance" exception to the warrant requirement.

c. Yes, because the agents exceeded the lawful scope of the premises search warrant by searching the vehicle that was not listed in the warrant.

d. Yes, because the agents did not have probable cause to believe that evidence of drug trafficking was located in the vehicle.

---

a. No, because it was found during the execution of a valid premises search warrant.
CORRECT: A search warrant authorizing a search of a certain premises includes any vehicles owned or controlled by the owner of the premises searched and located within its curtilage if the objects of the search might be located in those vehicles. In essence, the vehicle is treated as if it were part of the premises covered by the warrant. It should be remembered, however, that if the owner of the premises has a vehicle that is parked off the curtilage, it cannot be searched pursuant to the premises search warrant.

b. No, because the vehicle was searched pursuant to the "mobile conveyance" exception to the warrant requirement.
INCORRECT: The "mobile conveyance" exception to the Fourth Amendment's warrant requirement authorizes the search of a mobile conveyance if probable cause exists to believe it is carrying items subject to seizure (contraband, means and instrumentalities, etc.). In this case, the agents did not have probable cause, so the "mobile conveyance" exception was inapplicable.

c. Yes, because the agents exceeded the lawful scope of the premises search warrant by searching the vehicle that was not listed in the warrant.
INCORRECT: A search warrant authorizing a search of a certain premises includes any vehicles owned or controlled by the owner of the premises searched and located within its curtilage if the objects of the search might be located in those vehicles. In essence, the vehicle is treated as if it were part of the premises covered by the warrant. It should be remembered, however, that if the owner of the premises has a vehicle that is parked off the curtilage, it cannot be searched pursuant to the premises search warrant.

d. Yes, because the agents did not have probable cause to believe that evidence of drug trafficking was located in the vehicle.
INCORRECT: The agents did not need probable cause to believe that evidence of drug trafficking was located in the vehicle. A premises search warrant authorizes the search of any vehicles owned or controlled by the owner of the premises searched, and located within its curtilage, if the objects of the search might be located in those vehicles. In essence, the vehicle is treated as if it were part of the premises covered by the warrant.

28. Federal agents obtained an arrest warrant for Smith for bank fraud. Agents determine that Smith is single, lives alone, and is the only one at his residence. Agents lawfully enter Smith's house. They find Smith standing in the first floor entryway. Agent Brown does a protective sweep of the entryway coat closet and sees a shotgun as he opens the closet door. He seizes the shotgun knowing that Smith is a previously convicted felon and possession of a firearm by him is a federal offense. Agent Rogers does a protective sweep of the back, second floor bedroom and sees and seizes a stack of child pornographic magazines lying openly on top of the bed. Concerning the admissibility of the evidence seized:

a. Both the shotgun and the magazines are admissible.

b. Neither the shotgun nor the magazines are admissible.

c. The magazines are admissible. The shotgun is not.

d. The shotgun is admissible; the magazines are not.

---

a. Both the shotgun and the magazines are admissible.
INCORRECT: The search incident to arrest permits looking into the entry way closet because it was in an area immediately adjacent to the place of arrest and could conceal a person. The shotgun was lawfully seized in plain view. (Lawful presence, immediately apparent it was evidence of a crime, and lawful right to access.) The scope of the search incident to arrest was exceeded upstairs because there was no reasonable suspicion anyone was upstairs. Since the scope of the sweep was exceeded, the agent was not lawfully present in the bedroom making the plain view doctrine inapplicable.

b. Neither the shotgun nor the magazines are admissible.
INCORRECT: See justification a.

c. The magazines are admissible. The shotgun is not.
INCORRECT: See justification a.

d. The shotgun is admissible; the magazines are not.
CORRECT: See justification a.

29. Federal agents are conducting a surveillance of Johnson's house based on information that the house is being used to process and package cocaine. Agents standing on the public sidewalk look into Johnson's open living room window that is only 5 feet away. On the table in front of the window, agents see scales and bundles of what they immediately recognize as packaged cocaine. Agents knock on the door, Johnson answers, and the agents push their way in - without consent - and seize the cocaine. Concerning the admissibility of the evidence seized:

a. The cocaine is admissible because it was seen in plain view from a public place.

b. The cocaine is admissible because it was seized in plain view once agents entered the house.

c. The cocaine is inadmissible because the plain view doctrine does not apply to the seizure of the cocaine under the facts presented.

d. The cocaine is inadmissible because the "discovery" of the drugs was not inadvertent - the agents knew it was there before they entered the house.

---

a. The cocaine is admissible because it was seen in plain view from a public place.
INCORRECT: Though the agents were lawfully present when they saw the cocaine, and immediately recognized it as contraband, they had to have a lawful right to access the drugs to lawfully seize it. The information they obtained from the surveillance, however, could have been lawfully used to obtain a search warrant.

b. The cocaine is admissible because it was seized in plain view once agents entered the house.
INCORRECT: See justification a. Since the agents were not lawfully present when they seized the cocaine, the plain view doctrine does not apply.

c. The cocaine is inadmissible because the plain view doctrine does not apply to the seizure of the cocaine under the facts presented.
CORRECT: See justification a.

d. The cocaine is inadmissible because the "discovery" of the drugs was not inadvertent - the agents knew it was there before they entered the house.
INCORRECT: Inadvertence is no longer a prerequisite to a lawful plain view seizure. For example, assume that agents had probable cause to search for two contraband items (A and B), but obtained a search warrant for only item A. While lawfully present executing the search warrant for A, they see item B in plain view, and immediately recognize it as contraband. Item B could lawfully be seized under the plain view doctrine. The fact that they had PC (but no warrant) to search for B before entering does not destroy the applicability of the plain view doctrine.

30. Federal agents have been trying for weeks to catch Williams, who they have a hunch is manufacturing false identification cards. Frustrated with their lack of progress and the fact that Williams "is getting away with a crime," agents walk up the sidewalk to Williams' front door, knock, and identify themselves as agents. Pursuant to the agents' request to come in and talk, Williams admits the agents into the house, where they gather in the living room. One of the agents looks down on the floor and beside his foot is what he immediately recognizes as a marijuana cigarette. The agent retrieves the marijuana, signals the other agents to leave, and all the agents depart without arresting Williams. Concerning the admissibility of the cigarette the agent seized:

a. It is admissible because it was seized pursuant to the plain view doctrine.

b. It is admissible because the agents had consent to search the house.

c. It is inadmissible because the agents were in the house to discuss false identification documents, not a drug offense.

d. It is inadmissible because the agents did not arrest Williams when they found the cigarette.

---

a. It is admissible because it was seized pursuant to the plain view doctrine.
CORRECT: The agents were granted consent to enter the house. They were lawfully present in the living room when an agent saw the cigarette on the floor. The requirements of the plain view doctrine were met: lawful presence, immediately apparent the item was evidence of a crime or contraband, and a lawful right to access the evidence.

b. It is admissible because the agents had consent to search the house.
INCORRECT: See justification a. The agents did not search the house. In addition, the agents did not have consent to search it.

c. It is inadmissible because the agents were in the house to discuss false identification documents, not a drug offense.
INCORRECT: See justification a. What is important is that the agents were lawfully present when one saw what was immediately recognized as a marijuana cigarette. It doesn't matter that the reason they asked to come in was for a matter different than the type of criminal evidence one saw in plain view.

d. It is inadmissible because the agents did not arrest Williams when they found the cigarette.
INCORRECT: There is no requirement that officers arrest a defendant once probable cause develops.

31. Park Police officers see Ralston driving his car at an excessive speed on a park highway. Ralston is stopped for speeding and, during the investigation, the officers develop probable cause Ralston is driving while intoxicated. Ralston is arrested for that offense and his vehicle is towed to a secure, Park Police impoundment area. Pursuant to Park Police standardized policy to inventory all impounded vehicles within 24 hours, the officers inventory Ralston's car the next day. In the trunk they find a suitcase. They open the suitcase and discover a stash of counterfeit US currency. Concerning the admissibility of the currency in a court of law:

a. It is admissible because Ralston had been arrested, and this search incident to arrest permitted searching the suitcase.

b. It is admissible because the agents lawfully opened the suitcase.

c. It is inadmissible because the opening of the suitcase was not contemporaneous with the arrest.

d. It is inadmissible because the suitcase had nothing to do with the offense for which Ralston was arrested.

---

a. It is admissible because Ralston had been arrested, and this search incident to arrest permitted searching the suitcase.
INCORRECT: The suitcase was opened pursuant to an inventory, not a search incident to arrest. A search incident to arrest under these facts would not allow the officers to go into the trunk. In addition, a search incident to arrest must be substantially contemporaneous with the arrest.

b. It is admissible because the agents lawfully opened the suitcase.
CORRECT: This was a lawful inventory because there was a standardized policy. The officers did not exceed the scope of an inventory because the suitcase is a place where a person ordinarily stores personal property. Had the officers found the currency by cutting open a spare tire, for example, they would have exceeded the scope of the inventory because one does not ordinarily store personal property there.

c. It is inadmissible because the opening of the suitcase was not contemporaneous with the arrest.
INCORRECT: Did you confuse a search incident to arrest with an inventory? An SIA must be substantially contemporaneous with the arrest. Not so with an inventory, so long as it is conducted in accordance with a standardized agency policy.

d. It is inadmissible because the suitcase had nothing to do with the offense for which Ralston was arrested.
INCORRECT: The purpose of an inventory is not to conduct a criminal search for evidence. Inventories are permitted to protect the LEO and others from dangerous objects that may be present, to protect the owner's property, and to protect LEOs from false claims about damaged or missing property when the owner retrieves the property.

32. There is probable cause to arrest Jones for felony assault, but a warrant has not yet been issued. Officers call Jones at his home, verify that Jones is home, knock at the front door, announce their identity and purpose, and demand entry. While waiting for a reply, officers on the public street see what they immediately recognize to be a marijuana plant in the living room window. The officers receive no reply, so they force open the door and arrest Jones inside the house. During the protective sweep, they seize the plant they saw in the window. Concerning the admissibility of the marijuana plant at Jones's trial for possession of marijuana:

a. It is admissible because it was in open view from a public area and subject to seizure under the plain view doctrine.

b. It is admissible because the officers had probable cause to arrest, and they lawfully entered the house under hot pursuit.

c. It is not admissible because the protective sweep was unlawful.

d. It is not admissible because a protective sweep is limited to looking for people.

---

a. It is admissible because it was in open view from a public area and subject to seizure under the plain view doctrine.
INCORRECT: There was no arrest warrant and no authority (consent or hot pursuit) to enter Jones' house. This makes the protective sweep unlawful, and the fruits of the sweep will be suppressed. Though the officers saw the plant in open view from a public place, the facts provide no lawful right of access to the plant.

b. It is admissible because the officers had probable cause to arrest, and they lawfully entered the house under hot pursuit.
INCORRECT: The facts here do not support hot pursuit; Jones wasn't being pursued from a public place to a private one. The officers only knew that Jones was at home. This makes the protective sweep unlawful, and the fruits of the sweep will be suppressed.

c. It is not admissible because the protective sweep was unlawful.
CORRECT: See justification a. Because the entry was unlawful, the protective sweep was also unlawful. The officers were not lawfully present, making the plain view doctrine inapplicable.

d. It is not admissible because a protective sweep is limited to looking for people.
INCORRECT: See justification a. In addition, while a protective sweep is to look for people, anything discovered in plain view during a lawful protective sweep, which is immediately apparent to be the evidence of a crime, may be seized. Plain view will not apply here because the officers were not lawfully present.

5th and 6th Amendments Practice Exam

1. Officers arrest Fred and advise him of his <u>Miranda</u> rights. Fred understands his rights and verbally waives them. After 20 minutes of questioning, officers figure out that Fred is lying to them and so they tell Fred they will call the local Social Services office and have Fred's children taken away if Fred doesn't confess. Thereafter, Fred confesses. Was this confession obtained in violation of the 5th Amendment?

a. No, because Fred was given and waived his <u>Miranda</u> rights.

b. No, because Fred was not entitled to receive <u>Miranda</u> warnings.

c. Yes, because the statement was coerced.

d. Yes, because Fred didn't waive his <u>Miranda</u> rights in writing.

---

a. No, because Fred was given and waived his <u>Miranda</u> rights.
Incorrect: The statement was coerced. Coercion in obtaining a statement is contrary to the 5th Amendment even if the subject waives his <u>Miranda</u> rights.

b. No, because Fred was not entitled to receive <u>Miranda</u> warnings.
Incorrect: Fred was entitled to receive <u>Miranda</u> warnings because he was being interrogated by known police officers at a time when he was in custody (arrested).

c. Yes, because the statement was coerced.
Correct. Coercion in obtaining a statement is contrary to the 5th Amendment even if the subject waives his <u>Miranda</u> rights.

d. Yes, because Fred didn't waive his <u>Miranda</u> rights in writing.
Incorrect: A voluntary, intelligent, and knowing waiver of <u>Miranda</u> rights can be done verbally, though written waivers are best when they can be obtained.

2. Officers arrest Fred for larceny, advise him of his <u>Miranda</u> rights and obtain a valid waiver of them. As the questioning progresses, officers believe that Fred has not been truthful. They tell Fred that his fingerprints were found on the stolen items that were recovered; this is not true. They also tell Fred that if he cooperates in the investigation, the officers will tell the AUSA (federal prosecutor) that Fred was cooperative. Fred confesses to the larceny. Was this confession obtained in violation of the 5th Amendment?

a. No, because Fred waived his <u>Miranda</u> rights before being questioned by police.

b. No, because officers can say *anything* to get a suspect to confess.

c. Yes, because the police can't lie to a person being questioned.

d. Yes, because the statement about telling the AUSA about Fred's cooperation was improper.

---

a. No, because Fred waived his <u>Miranda</u> rights before being questioned by police.
Correct. (Be sure to read the justifications for the below, incorrect answers.)

b. No, because officers can say *anything* to get a suspect to confess.
Incorrect: While there was no 5th Amendment violation here, police cannot threaten or coerce a person. Also, if the interrogation technique is such that a person's free will in making a statement is overborne, that too would result in a 5th Amendment violation. That was not the case here.

c. Yes, because the police can't lie to a person being questioned.
Incorrect: Police are allowed to use trickery and deception during questioning to get to the truth, so long as the suspect's will is not overborne. Such practices, however, can NOT be used in obtaining a <u>Miranda</u> waiver.

d. Yes, because the statement about telling the AUSA about Fred's cooperation was improper.
Incorrect: There is nothing improper in letting Fred know that if he cooperates, his cooperation will be made known to the AUSA. Telling Fred that if he confessed that his sentence or the severity of the charges would be reduced, however, would be improper.

5th and 6th Amendments Practice Exam

3. Fred is arrested for making harassing phone calls and is in custody. Some of the calls were recorded. Officers want a voice exemplar (sample) of Fred's voice to compare Fred's voice to the recordings. Without giving Fred <u>Miranda</u> rights, officers obtain a subpoena and court order directing Fred to give the voice exemplar. Can Fred be required to provide the voice exemplar over his objection?

a. No, because the exemplar might incriminate Fred.

b. No, because before the police can lawfully ask *any* questions of a person in custody, the suspect must first be given, and waive, his <u>Miranda</u> rights.

c. Yes, because once a person is in custody, they no longer have to be given <u>Miranda</u> rights.

d. Yes, because giving the exemplar is not protected by the 5th Amendment.

---

a. No, because the exemplar might incriminate Fred.
Incorrect: While the results of the exemplar might be used at Fred's trial to convict him, the exemplar is "non-testimonial" and therefore not protected by the 5th Amendment.

b. No, because before the police can lawfully ask *any* questions of a person in custody, the suspect must first be given, and waive, his <u>Miranda</u> rights.
Incorrect: This statement is too broad to be correct. Booking, and public and officer safety, questions of a person, for example, do not require <u>Miranda</u>.

c. Yes, because once a person is in custody, they no longer have to be given <u>Miranda</u> rights.
Incorrect: Those in custody generally do have to be given and waive <u>Miranda</u> rights if they are to be questioned by the police. (Those not in custody do not have such rights.) There are exceptions. See the above answer.

d. Yes, because giving the exemplar is not protected by the 5th Amendment.
Correct: The exemplar is "non-testimonial" and therefore not protected by the 5th Amendment.

4. Based on reasonable suspicion that Jack is a bank robber they are looking for, officers perform a <u>Terry</u> stop at gun point, put him on the ground, handcuff him, perform a <u>Terry</u> frisk, and place him in the back seat of the patrol vehicle. 25 minutes later, the officers leave the scene and transport him to the office downtown. 15 minutes later when they arrive at the office, officers leave Jack in the cruiser and in cuffs, and then begin to question him. At this time, officers have not placed Jack under arrest, and they have not given Jack <u>Miranda</u> warnings. Jack confesses. Was this confession obtained in violation of <u>Miranda</u>?

a. No, because Jack wasn't under arrest and therefore not in custody for <u>Miranda</u> purposes.

b. No, because Jack wasn't booked into a jail cell before being questioned.

c. Yes, because Jack was in custody for purposes of <u>Miranda</u>.

d. Yes, because <u>Miranda</u> warnings are required whenever one who is the subject of a <u>Terry</u> stop is questioned.

---

a. No, because Jack wasn't under arrest and therefore not in custody for <u>Miranda</u> purposes.
Incorrect: While Jack was not formally arrested, a reasonable person would conclude they were under arrest in these circumstances and therefore in custody for <u>Miranda</u> purposes.

b. No, because Jack wasn't booked into a jail cell before being questioned.
Incorrect: A person doesn't have to be physically in a jail cell before <u>Miranda</u> is triggered. Formal arrest, or the functional equivalent of arrest, is sufficient to trigger <u>Miranda</u>.

c. Yes, because Jack was in custody for purposes of <u>Miranda</u>.
Correct: While the officers might have intended only a <u>Terry</u> stop, the facts here would lead a reasonable person to believe they were under arrest given the length of time Jack was detained, the manner in which the stop was conducted, the time Jack was in restraints, and the fact that he was transported from the scene.

d. Yes, because <u>Miranda</u> warnings are required whenever one who is the subject of a <u>Terry</u> stop is questioned.
Incorrect: This statement is incorrect. In most cases, <u>Terry</u> stops are not "custody" for the purposes of <u>Miranda</u> and therefore do not require <u>Miranda</u> warnings.

5. Fred was arrested for selling counterfeit currency shortly after an undercover buy operation and a brief chase down a street. The arresting officer immediately performed a search incident to arrest, but was surprised to find that Fred did not have the "buy money" on his person. Without advising Fred of his <u>Miranda</u> rights, the officer said "Okay, Fred, show me where the money is." Fred then pointed to some bushes 200 feet away next to the sidewalk where he had been chased, and the marked "buy money" was found there. Was this information obtained from Fred in violation of <u>Miranda</u>?

a. No, because Fred wasn't questioned or interrogated.

b. No, because Fred wasn't in a jail setting and therefore not in custody.

c. Yes, because the officer did not obtain a valid <u>Miranda</u> waiver.

d. Yes, because <u>Miranda</u> rights are required before asking *any* questions of a person who has been arrested.

---

a. No, because Fred wasn't questioned or interrogated.
Incorrect: Fred was being questioned. See the justification for question c.

b. No, because Fred wasn't in a jail setting and therefore not in custody.
Incorrect: Fred was under arrest and that constitutes "custody" for purposes of <u>Miranda</u>.

c. Yes, because the officer did not obtain a valid <u>Miranda</u> waiver.
Correct: Whenever a known officer interrogates a person in custody, <u>Miranda</u> rights must first be given and a valid waiver obtained. Fred was under arrest by an officer. Law enforcement questioning includes not only asking questions that might elicit a criminal response, but any conduct that might do so. The officer's statement to Fred is likely to elicit a criminal response (pointing). Accordingly, <u>Miranda</u> rights, and a valid waiver, were required before having Fred point to the money's location.

d. Yes, because <u>Miranda</u> rights are required before asking *any* questions of a person who has been arrested.
Incorrect: This is an incorrect statement. Officer and public safety questions, and booking questions, for example, do not require <u>Miranda</u> warnings and waiver even if the person has been arrested.

6. Jack is arrested for assaulting Jill. As soon as Jack is arrested, and during the search incident to arrest and before Jack is read his <u>Miranda</u> rights, Jack screams out to the police, "Arrest me if you want to, but Jill got what she deserved." The officers then ask Jack his full name, date of birth, and SSN. Jack provides the information. Which, if either, of the statements that Jack made were obtained in violation of <u>Miranda?</u>

a. Both statements (#1: what Jack screamed out, and #2, the information regarding his name, DOB, and SSN).

b. The first statement only.

c. The second statement only.

d. Neither statement.

---

a. Both statements (#1: what Jack screamed out, and #2, the information regarding his name, DOB, and SSN).
Incorrect: See the justification to answer d.

b. The first statement only.
Incorrect: See the justification to answer d.

c. The second statement only.
Incorrect: See the justification to answer d.

d. Neither statement.
Correct: The first statement was spontaneous on Jack's part and not the result of law enforcement questioning. The second statement also did not constitute questioning (interrogation) under <u>Miranda</u> as it was a proper booking question.

7. Officers develop probable cause that Fred just attempted to rob a Wal-Mart at gun-point and is still inside the store. The officers find Fred and arrest him in the store. During the search incident to arrest, the officers do not find a gun. An officer asks, "Where is the gun?" and Fred says, "Over by the fishing reels." The gun is found where Fred said it was. The officer then asks, "Is this the gun that you used to try and rob this store?" Fred answers "Yes." At no time was Fred given Miranda warnings. Which of these statements was obtained in violation of Miranda?

a. Both statements.

b. Neither statement.

c. The first statement ("by the fishing reels") but not the second.

d. The second statement ("yes") but not the first.

---

a. Both statements.
Incorrect: See the justification to answer d.

b. Neither statement.
Incorrect: See the justification to answer d.

c. The first statement ("by the fishing reels") but not the second.
Incorrect: See the justification to answer d.

d. The second statement ("yes") but not the first.
Correct: The first question was a proper officer safety question. Although it produced an incriminating response, the question was not designed to elicit an incriminating response but for public safety because the officers had reason to believe the gun was somewhere in the store. (A proper officer safety question can also include asking an arrestee, "Do you have any weapons or objects on you that might hurt me?") Officer and public safety questions do not require Miranda warnings. The second question is not related to officer or public safety, but instead designed to elicit an incriminating response. That question required Miranda warnings and waiver.

8. Officers arrest Fred for larceny. When giving Fred his Miranda warnings, they tell Fred he has been arrested for larceny. Fred waives his Miranda rights and talks to officers. During the course of the interview, the officers realize that Fred is not only a thief, but also possessed a small amount of marijuana (a misdemeanor). They ask him questions about his drug possession to which Fred confesses. Were Fred's statements about his drug possession obtained in violation of Miranda?

a. No, because officers had a proper Miranda waiver.

b. No, because Miranda warnings are not required when officers question a person in custody about a misdemeanor.

c. Yes, because Fred was arrested for larceny and not drug possession.

d. Yes, because the Miranda warnings Fred was given did not mention drug possession.

---

a. No, because officers had a proper Miranda waiver.
Correct: Officers may, but are not required, to tell a suspect the offenses about which they intend to ask questions. Once Fred waived his Miranda rights, officers may question him about any offense.

b. No, because Miranda warnings are not required when law enforcement questions a person in custody about a misdemeanor.
Incorrect: There is no such rule of law.

c. Yes, because Fred was arrested for larceny and not drug possession.
Incorrect: See the justification to answer a.

d. Yes, because the Miranda warnings Fred was given did not mention drug possession.
Incorrect: See the justification to answer a.

9. Based upon reasonable suspicion that Fred is involved in a larceny, officers Terry stop Fred. As soon as the officers approach, Fred says, "Don't bother asking me any questions. I have a lawyer." After some more investigation the officers develop probable cause that Fred committed the larceny. The officers arrest Fred 10 minutes later and take him to the office. There the officers read Fred his Miranda rights which Fred waives. Fred confesses to the larceny. Did the officer's actions violate Miranda?

a. Yes, because Fred invoked his right to silence.

b. Yes, because Fred invoked his right to counsel.

c. No, because one cannot invoke Miranda rights in anticipation of the arrest.

d. No, because officers should have Mirandized Fred when they made the Terry stop.

---

a. Yes, because Fred invoked his right to silence.
Incorrect: One can not validly invoke their right to silence in anticipation of interrogation and before Miranda rights are given.

b. Yes, because Fred invoked his right to counsel.
Incorrect: One can not validly invoke their right to silence in anticipation of interrogation and before Miranda rights are given. In addition, the "request" for counsel was ambiguous.

c. No, because one cannot invoke Miranda rights in anticipation of the arrest.
Correct: See the justifications to answers a and b above.

d. No, because officers should have Mirandized Fred when they made the Terry stop.
Incorrect: Questioning of a person after a Terry stop, and where the stop is not the functional equivalent of an arrest, does not require Miranda.

10. Fred is arrested for arson. After being read his _Miranda_ rights, Fred says, "I don't want to talk to law enforcement." The officers immediately end their attempt to question Fred and return him to his jail cell awaiting his initial appearance in the morning. About 2 hours later as the officers get ready to leave, they stop by Fred's cell and ask him if he would like to talk to them. Fred says he does want to talk, and the officers re-advise Fred of his _Miranda_ rights all of which Fred validly waives. Fred confesses. Did the officer's actions violate _Miranda?_

a. Yes, because once Fred invoked, the officers may not attempt to question Fred until he is released from custody.

b. Yes, because the statement Fred made was coerced.

c. No, because the officers can see if Fred changed his mind about talking to them anytime the officers want to.

d. No, because the officers were permitted to re-approach Fred.

---

a. Yes, because once Fred invoked, the officers may not attempt to question Fred until he is released from custody.
Incorrect: Because Fred invoked only his right to silence, and not counsel, officers may approach after a suitable cooling-off period to see if Fred has changed his mind.

b. Yes, because the statement Fred made was coerced.
Incorrect: There are no facts that would indicate that Fred was coerced into talking with the officers.

c. No, because the officers can see if Fred changed his mind about talking to them anytime the officers want to.
Incorrect: This statement is too broad. See the justification to answer a.

d. No, because the officers were permitted to re-approach Fred.
Correct. See the justification to answer a.

11. Fred is arrested for arson. After being read his <u>Miranda</u> rights, Fred says, "I want a lawyer." The officers stop the attempt to question Fred. Consistent with <u>Miranda,</u> under which of the following circumstances may the officers again attempt to question Fred? (Assume Fred has no 6th Amendment right to counsel.)

a. Once Fred has had a chance to speak with a lawyer.

b. After a suitable cooling off period.

c. Once Fred is released from custody or initiates questioning on his own.

d. A different set of officers attempt to question Fred or to question him about a different offense.

---

a. Once Fred has had a chance to speak with a lawyer.
Incorrect: The <u>Miranda</u> right is to have one's lawyer *present*.

b. After a suitable cooling off period.
Incorrect: If Fred had only invoked his right to silence, this answer would be correct. If a suspect requests a lawyer after being <u>Mirandized,</u> officers may not re-initiate questioning unless the suspect's lawyer is present.

c. Once Fred is released from custody or initiates questioning on his own.
Correct: <u>Miranda</u> applies only to those in custody. In addition, Fred could reinitiate the questioning on his own, and if he did, he could be lawfully questioned if he then waived his <u>Miranda</u> rights.

d. A different set of officers attempt to question Fred or to question him about a different offense.
Incorrect: So long as Fred remains in custody, his request for counsel must scrupulously honored as to ANY offense by ANY officers unless his lawyer is present or Fred re-initiates questioning.

12. Fred is arrested for shoplifting at the FLETC Express store (a misdemeanor). He validly waives his <u>Miranda</u> rights. About an hour into the interview, Fred realizes things are more serious than he thought and he says to the officers, "A lawyer might be a good idea." May the officers continue questioning Fred?

a. Yes, because Fred did not invoke his right to counsel.

b. Yes, because a request for counsel after the interview has begun is too late.

c. No, because the officers did not clarify what Fred meant by the statement.

d. No, because a request for counsel in a misdemeanor case does not have to be honored.

---

a. Yes, because Fred did not invoke his right to counsel.
Correct. Fred's statement is not considered to be an effective assertion of the right to counsel because it was ambiguous (unclear). See also the justification to answer c.

b. Yes, because a request for counsel after the interview has begun is too late.
Incorrect: A person can invoke their right to counsel, or silence, at any time.

c. No, because the officers did not clarify what Fred meant by the statement.
Incorrect: While the Supreme Court has said that clarification of the statement is a "good police practice," clarification is not required under the law.

d. No, because a request for counsel in a misdemeanor case does not have to be honored.
Incorrect: There is no such rule of law.

13. Fred is arrested and is placed into a physical line-up to see if witnesses can identify him as the perpetrator. This line-up violates either <u>Miranda</u> or the 5th Amendment due process provision if:

a. Officers fail to give Fred his <u>Miranda</u> rights and obtain a waiver.

b. It is a "show-up" line-up conducted right after the crime was allegedly committed and near the place of the alleged crime.

c. Fred refuses to participate in the line-up.

d. In a line-up with 5 other people, Fred is at least 6 inches taller than any of the others.

---

a. Officers fail to give Fred his <u>Miranda</u> rights and obtain a waiver.
Incorrect: Under these circumstances, no <u>Miranda</u> warnings or waiver are required because Fred is not being interrogated by law enforcement, and his being in the line-up is not testimonial.

b. It is a "show-up" line-up conducted right after the crime was allegedly committed and near the place of the alleged crime.
Incorrect: While show-up line-ups are not favored under the law, such a line-up conducted near the time and place of the crime are acceptable if not otherwise unduly suggestive.

c. Fred refuses to participate in the line-up.
Incorrect: Fred cannot refuse to participate in the line-up. To make Fred participate against his will, however, would require a subpoena or court order.

d. In a line-up with 5 other people, Fred is at least 6 inches taller than any of the others.
Correct: A line-up procedure cannot be "unduly suggestive." Line-ups where the participants are very dissimilar in appearance are unduly suggestive.

5th and 6th Amendments Practice Exam

14. The Jones Corporation is under investigation for fraud. Agents have reason to believe that the corporation possesses documents that will show it is engaged in the fraud. The agents obtain a subpoena for the records and serve it on Mrs. Smith, the records custodian. Is Smith's claim that producing the records might violate the corporations 5th Amendment right against self-incrimination valid?

a. Yes, because the records might incriminate Smith.

b. Yes, because the records might incriminate the corporation.

c. No, because the corporation does not have a 5th Amendment privilege against self-incrimination.

d. No, because the agents could have obtained the information with a warrant anyway.

---

a. Yes, because the records might incriminate Smith.
Incorrect: The subpoena is directed for the corporate records, and the corporation does not have a 5th Amendment privilege against self-incrimination. If the records would tend to incriminate Smith personally, the government would not be allowed to use the fact that Smith is the one that produced the records (act of production immunity).

b. Yes, because the records might incriminate the corporation.
Incorrect: The corporation does not have a 5th Amendment privilege against self-incrimination.

c. No, because the corporation does not have a 5th Amendment privilege against self-incrimination.
Correct: The corporation does not have a 5th Amendment privilege against self-incrimination.

d. No, because the agents could have obtained the information with a warrant anyway.
Incorrect: This is not relevant. The corporation does not have a 5th Amendment privilege against self-incrimination, though they do have rights under the 4th Amendment.

15. Fred and four of his friends rob a bank, but only Fred is arrested. Agents want Fred to provide information about the other four robbers. Fred invokes both his right to silence and counsel. Agents arrange with the AUSA and obtain use immunity for Fred for his involvement in the robbery. They then subpoena Fred to testify before the grand jury and a subsequent trial. Which of the following is true about this grant of immunity?

a. Fred can not be prosecuted for bank robbery.

b. Fred can not be prosecuted for perjury should he lie before the grand jury or at the trial.

c. Fred still has a Fifth Amendment privilege against self-incrimination concerning the bank robbery.

d. Evidence discovered or derived from Fred's testimony can not be used against Fred if he is prosecuted for any offense.

---

a. Fred can not be prosecuted for bank robbery.
Incorrect: Because Fred was only given use, and not transactional, immunity, he can be prosecuted for the bank robbery.

b. Fred can not be prosecuted for perjury should he lie before the grand jury or at the trial.
Incorrect: A grant of immunity is not a license to lie. If Fred lies under oath, he can be prosecuted for perjury. In addition, if he lies to agents, he could be prosecuted for false statement, 18 USC Section 1001.

c. Fred still has a Fifth Amendment privilege against self-incrimination concerning the bank robbery.
Incorrect: Because the testimony Fred is being compelled to give can no longer be used in a criminal proceeding, the grant of immunity has extinguished Fred's 5th Amendment right against self-incrimination as to the bank robbery.

d. Evidence discovered or derived from Fred's testimony can not be used against Fred if he is prosecuted for any offense.
Correct: Use immunity prohibits the government from using not only Fred's testimony against him, but information derived or discovered as a result of the immunized testimony. If the information Fred gave pursuant to the grant of immunity was already known to the government, it could be used.

16. Fred is a federal employee suspected of harassing another agency employee in the government workplace. Special Agent Jones of the agency's Office of Inspector General is conducting an internal investigation of Fred. Fred is called to an interview is held in Jones' office. Fred is not under arrest and the setting is non-custodial. Fred is advised at the outset of the interview that he is obligated to answer the agent's questions concerning the misconduct, but that his answers and any information derived from his answers cannot be used against him in a criminal case. Which of the following is true?

a. If Fred refuses to answer the questions by asserting his 5th Amendment privilege, he cannot be fired by the agency solely for that refusal.

b. If Fred admits to engaging in misconduct, the admission could be used to fire him, but not to prosecute him criminally.

c. If Fred lies to Special Agent Jones, his false statements cannot be used to criminally prosecute him for making false statements.

d. Because Fred is being compelled, under threat of possible firing, to answer the questions, any answers he gives would be obtained in violation of his 5th Amendment privilege and could not be used to either fire or prosecute him.

---

a. If Fred refuses to answer the questions by asserting his 5th Amendment privilege, he cannot be fired by the agency solely for that refusal.
Incorrect: By virtue of the use immunity conferred by SA Jones (called *Kalkines* immunity), Fred has no valid 5th Amendment privilege to assert (no possibility he can incriminate himself). Fred's unprivileged refusal to cooperate with an agency internal investigation is a violation of his obligation as a public employee, and he can be fired by his agency for that violation.

b. If Fred admits to engaging in harassment, the admission could be used to fire him for harassment, but not to prosecute him criminally.
Correct: The use immunity provided to Fred precludes use of his responses to criminally prosecute him. However, the immunity is limited to barring use in a criminal proceeding and does not bar use in an administrative disciplinary proceeding.

c. If Fred lies to Special Agent Jones, his false statements cannot be used to criminally prosecute him for making false statements.
Incorrect: The use immunity given to Fred does not permit him to engage in a new crime (lying to a federal officer in an official matter). Fred's false statements can be used to criminally prosecute him for the false statements offense.

d. Because Fred is being compelled, under threat of possible firing, to answer the questions, any answers he gives would be obtained in violation of his 5th Amendment privilege and could not be used to either fire or prosecute him.
Incorrect: See a. and b. above.

17. Fred has been indicted for larceny and is not in custody. He has not asserted his right to counsel. Federal Agent Jones wants to talk to Fred about the larceny, plus another crime, arson. As to the arson, Fred has not been indicted, has not made an initial appearance, and the AUSA has not filed an information. Which of the following is a true statement?

a. Jones must get a waiver of <u>Miranda</u> rights before he can question Fred about *either* offense.

b. Jones must get a waiver of 6th Amendment rights before he talks to Fred about the arson.

c. Jones must get a waiver of 6th Amendment rights before he talks to Fred about the larceny.

d. Jones must get a waiver of 6th Amendment rights before he talks to Fred about *either* the larceny or the arson.

---

a. Jones must get a waiver of <u>Miranda</u> rights before he can question Fred about *either* offense.
Incorrect: Fred is not in custody so <u>Miranda</u> is not triggered for either offense.

b. Jones must get a waiver of 6th Amendment rights before he talks to Fred about the arson.
Incorrect: Because Fred has not been indicted or made an initial appearance for the arson, and the AUSA has not filed an information, Fred's 6th Amendment right to counsel has not been triggered.

c. Jones must get a waiver of 6th Amendment rights before he talks to Fred about the larceny.
Correct: Fred's 6th Amendment right has been triggered because he has been indicted. Furthermore, law enforcement questioning (as well as being physically placed into a line-up or being in court for the charged offense) are critical stages. Since the 6th Amendment has been triggered and the questioning is a critical stage, Jones must first obtain a waiver of Fred's 6th Amendment right to counsel. This would be accomplished by using the same form and waiver as is used in a <u>Miranda</u> situation.

d. Jones must get a waiver of 6th Amendment rights before he talks to Fred about *either* the larceny or the arson.
Incorrect: See the justification to answers b and c. Remember that 6th Amendment rights (unlike <u>Miranda</u> rights) are offense specific, that is, are triggered only for the offense for which the subject has been indicted, made an initial appearance, or an information filed.

18. Fred has been indicted for larceny and is in jail awaiting his initial appearance. He has not asserted his right to counsel. Agents decide they want to have an undercover officer pretend to be a fellow prisoner, get close to Fred, and report back any relevant information. Which of the following is correct?

a. Because Fred is in custody, he must first waive his <u>Miranda</u> rights before being questioned.

b. The undercover officer can attempt to question Fred about larceny without first obtaining a waiver of <u>Miranda</u> or the 6th Amendment right to counsel.

c. The undercover officer may listen to whatever Fred says but may not attempt to question Fred about the larceny.

d. It is unlawful for agents to ask other inmates what they might have heard Fred say about the larceny.

---

a. Because Fred is in custody, he must first waive his <u>Miranda</u> rights before being questioned.
Incorrect: Because the questioning would be done by one whom Fred did not know was a law enforcement officer, <u>Miranda</u> warnings are not required.

b. The undercover officer can attempt to question Fred about larceny without first obtaining a waiver of <u>Miranda</u> or the 6th Amendment right to counsel.
Incorrect: See the justifications to answers a and c.

c. The undercover officer may listen to whatever Fred says but may not attempt to question Fred about the larceny.
Correct: Because Fred has been indicted, his 6th Amendment right to counsel has attached. Because the questioning will be done by (or at the behest of) law enforcement, it is a critical stage. Accordingly, a 6th Amendment waiver is required before questioning Fred.

If Fred had not been indicted, made an initial appearance, or there was no information filed, agents could lawfully use an undercover agent or confidential informant to question Fred without getting a waiver of any rights. Fred's 6th Amendment rights had not attached. Though Fred is in custody, he would not have <u>Miranda</u> rights because he would not questioned by one he knew was a law enforcement officer. An undercover agent or a confidential informant working for law enforcement, however, may act as a "listening post" to passively gather information.

d. It is unlawful for agents to ask other inmates what they might have heard Fred say about the larceny.
Incorrect: Though Fred's 6th Amendment rights have attached, he is not being questioned by, or at the behest, of law enforcement. Agents may use inmates, undercover agents, or confidential informants just listen to, but not question, Fred.

Courtroom Evidence Practice Exam

1. Which of the following correctly describes what a jury may do if evidence is suppressed?

A. The jury may fully consider evidence that is suppressed.

B. The jury may not consider evidence that is suppressed.

C. The jury may consider evidence that is suppressed, but cannot give it the same, full consideration as other evidence.

D. The jury may not consider evidence that is suppressed, but the lawyers may refer to it as "evidence in the case."

Correct Answer: B. A suppression hearing is held in the presence of the judge. The jury is not present. If the evidence is suppressed, that means that the evidence is not admissible and the jury will not know about that evidence. Since the evidence is not admitted, the lawyers cannot refer to it in the case.

_____

2. What occurs after there is an objection to evidence at a trial?

A. Because there is an objection, the evidence will not be admitted.

B. Because there is an objection, the evidence will be admitted.

C. If the judge sustains the objection, the evidence will be admitted.

D. If the judge overrules the objection, the evidence will be admitted.

Correct Answer D. When there is an objection to evidence, the judge must rule on the objection. When an objection is sustained (the judge agrees to the objection), the evidence will not be admitted. If the judge sustains the objection (agrees to the objection,) the evidence is not admitted. A jury cannot consider evidence when the judge sustains an objection.

_____

3. The U.S. Government is prosecuting a murderer who killed some doctors. During the trial, the AUSA plans to offer a weapon, found at the scene and registered to the defendant. In order to get the weapon admitted into evidence, the AUSA must:

A. Offer the testimony of a witness that the weapon was recovered at the scene.

B. Offer a picture of the weapon to save time.

C. Not offer the murder weapon unless the defendant takes the stand and admits that it is his weapon.

D. Not offer the murder weapon since the only way to get the rifle admitted is through the testimony of an expert witness.

Correct Answer: A. A the party offering an item into evidence is required to lay a foundation for it. A proper foundation consists of evidence, usually in the form of testimony, that the item is what the party offering it claims it to be. In this case, a foundation is laid through the testimony of a witness who can testify from personal knowledge that the exhibit being offered in court is the one they saw, seized, or collected. Answer B is not correct, because, while the photo might be admitted, it won't get the weapon admitted. Answer C is incorrect because it is not a requirement that the defendant take the stand and admit it is his weapon. In fact the defendant has the right not to take the stand and testify. Answer D is incorrect because it is not a requirement that an expert testify in order to lay a foundation for this evidence.

---

4. Evidence was seized during the execution of a search warrant. If a chain of custody is properly prepared for the item, does that eliminate the need to lay a foundation?

A. Yes, a proper chain of custody satisfies all admissibility requirements.

B. Yes, provided that the person who seized the evidence is the first person on the chain of custody form.

C. No, a foundation is still required.

D. No, the seizure of the evidence must be attested to by a corroborating witness.

Correct Answer: C. For physical evidence to be admissible in court, there must be a showing that it is authentic, that is, some evidence the item is what its proponent claims it to be. In court, the process of authenticating the evidence is called "laying the foundation." A foundation is laid by the AUSA based on facts collected by officers and agents. A foundation can be laid in two ways. The first way is to have a witness testify as to their personal knowledge. In the case of seized evidence, this will usually be the officer who first seized the evidence. The other method of authentication is through self-authentication for public records and reports or business records. Even when a proper foundation is laid, it is still necessary to be able to fend off claims of alterations to the evidence or mishandling. That is the purpose of the chain of custody. Answer C is the correct answer because even if the chain of custody is correct, a foundation must still be laid in court. Answer A is incorrect because a chain of custody does not satisfy authentication requirements. Answer B is incorrect because even though the first person on the chain of custody is usually the person who seized the evidence (and would lay the foundation in court), the foundation must still actually be laid in court with that witness testifying. Answer D is incorrect because there is no rule that the seizure of evidence must be attested to by a corroborating witness.

5. Despite his checkered past, Cynthia decided to marry Mark. On their honeymoon to Las Vegas, she saw him brazenly steal a vending machine with $1,000 of postage stamps inside. Although he never talked to his wife about the crime, Mark's new family obligations led him to talk to his psychotherapist about the crime during therapy and confess it to his priest as well. After being caught, he told the whole story to the lawyer appointed to represent him at his initial appearance. Not liking that lawyer's advice, Mark fired her and hired another lawyer. On the morning of his federal trial, he sees his wife, his psychotherapist, his priest and his first lawyer entering the prosecution witness waiting room. Which witness is he least likely to be able to prevent from testifying by solely by applying the law of privileges?

A. His wife.

B. His psychotherapist.

C. His priest.

D. His first lawyer.

Correct Answer: A. (His wife.) Cynthia can refuse to testify against her husband. If Cynthia waives that privilege, she will be allowed to testify about what she saw (but not about what Mark may have told her.) Mark can prevent testimony about his admissions to his psychotherapist and his priest since he is the holder of these privileges. He can also prevent his first lawyer from testifying about their confidential communications, even though he later fired that lawyer.

————————

6. A 22-year-old son is visiting his mother and father. While sorting his laundry, his mother finds a suspicious vial of pills in his pants pocket. She takes them to the police. They do a field test that proves positive for cocaine, initiate a chain of custody document, and send it to the lab. The laboratory confirms the pills are tabletized cocaine. On the day of trial of the son for drug possession, which problem would be the hardest for the prosecutor to overcome?

A. The mother's assertion of the parent-child privilege.

B. The father's asserting of the spousal privilege to prevent the wife and mother from testifying to the circumstances surrounding her discovery of the cocaine.

C. The mother's failure to appear at trial.

D. The failure to produce documents relating to the original field test of the cocaine.

Correct Answer: C. The parent-child privilege is not recognized in federal court. The spousal privilege is not applicable on these facts. The loss of documentation concerning the original field test is problematic, but not fatal so long as chain of custody and laboratory confirmation of the cocaine can be established. But if the mother is not available to testify, a proper foundation for introduction of the drugs as being found in the son's clothing cannot be laid, and the case is likely to be dismissed.

————————

7. George Gabs has been serving as a government informant for DEA on a federal cocaine trafficking case in California. George Gabs' information has been so reliable that DEA agents have successfully made a trafficking cocaine case against a network of fifteen defendants. During pretrial hearings, Defense counsel informs the judge that one of the pending defense motions before the court is to require the government to reveal the informant's identity so that defense counsel can adequately prepare a defense for trial. Who holds the privilege?

A. As a government employee, the agent holds the privilege.

B. The informant holds the privilege.

C. The defense attorney holds the privilege.

D. The AUSA holds the privilege on behalf of the U. S. Government.

Correct Answer: D. The government-informant privilege is different in two respects: (a) what is privileged is not the communication, but the identity of the informant and information that would reveal the informant's identity, and (b) the holder of the privilege is not the person who made the communication, but to whom the communication was made (the government). The government holds this privilege and the AUSA, on behalf of the government, is the one who decides whether or not to waive it. A judge may require the AUSA to reveal the informant's identify if that would be helpful and relevant to the defense's case. If the judge decides that the informant's identity should be revealed, the AUSA must either do so or dismiss the case. Since the agent is not the holder of the privilege, answer A is incorrect. Since the informant is not the holder of the privilege, answer B is incorrect. Since the defense attorney is not the holder of the privilege, answer C is incorrect.

––––––––––

8. Officer Jones is on-duty when a citizen walks up and says, "Officer, a friend told me there are some people trying to break into a building down the street." May the officer lawfully use the information she received from the citizen?

A. No, because what the friend said is hearsay.

B. No, because the reports of citizens on the street are unreliable.

C. Yes, she may consider the information because the hearsay rule applies only at trials.

D. Yes, she may consider the information because even though it is hearsay, there is an exception that applies.

Correct Answer C. With the exception of privileges (like the attorney-client privilege, for example) the rules of evidence apply only to trials. When an officer receives information on the street, he is not in trial and the hearsay rule does not apply.

––––––––––

9. The prosecution in a robbery case is trying to prove that the defendant is the person who robbed the victim. Which one of the following is an example of circumstantial evidence to prove this point?

A. The victim testifies, "The defendant stuck a gun in my face and demanded money."

B. A witness testifies, "I saw the defendant point a gun at the victim."

C. A police officer testifies, "I asked the defendant if he robbed the victim and the defendant said yes."

D. A witness testifies that the defendant's gun was found near the scene of the robbery soon after the robbery occurred.

Correct Answer: D. Answers A through C are all direct evidence. In other words, they tend to prove the matter in question directly without the use of an inference or deduction. Answer D is circumstantial evidence. It does not prove the robbery directly, but may do so indirectly though an inference that if the defendant's gun was found near the robbery scene soon after the robbery, the defendant might have been the robber.

---

10. Joe Madman entered the First National Bank of Florida to commit an armed robbery. He was dressed in all black and wearing a red bandanna which covered the lower portion of his facial area during the robbery. He rushed up to the bank teller and demanded, "Give me all your money. Put it in my bag now or I'll blow your head off!" The teller could see he had a black Glock pointed at her head. The teller recognized his distinct voice immediately. Not only was he a regular customer, but he also sang in the church choir with her. After Joe Madman was apprehended, he was tried for armed robbery. At trial will the bank teller be able to testify she recognized the defendant's voice?

A. Yes, because she is familiar with it. Her lay witness testimony is acceptable.

B. No, because she is not allowed to give her opinion since she is not an expert.

C. Yes, but only if Madman testifies at trial.

D. No, because identifications can not be based upon voice recognition.

Correct Answer: A. A lay witness can give an opinion when: (a) the opinion is rationally based on the witness' perception and personal knowledge, (b) the opinion is helpful to a clear understanding of the witness' testimony or the determination of a fact in issue, and (c) the opinion is not one that is based on scientific, technical, or other specialized knowledge. Some examples of a proper lay witness opinion include: identification of handwriting, and voices, provided that the witness is sufficiently familiar with them. A lay witness could also testify as to a person's emotional conditions.

---

11. Susie is on trial for forging prescriptions for oxycontin, a controlled substance. The nurse that works as office manager for the doctor, whose prescription pad was stolen by Susie, is one of the prosecution's main witnesses. In order to prove that it is Susie's handwriting which appears on the forged prescriptions, the prosecutor calls her brother, Tom, who is to testify that he is familiar with Susie's handwriting, and the writing on the prescription is definitely his sister's. Is this testimony admissible?

A. Yes, because, the witness has sufficient familiarity with his sister's handwriting.

B. No, because, the witness must be qualified as an expert.

C. Yes, because, anyone may testify as to handwriting.

D. No, because the witness is the defendant's brother and he may be biased.

Correct Answer: A. A lay witness may give an opinion only when (a) the opinion is rationally based on the witness' perception and personal knowledge, (b) the opinion is helpful to a clear understanding of the witness' testimony or the determination of a fact is issue, and (c) the opinion is not one that is based on scientific, technical, or other specialized knowledge. Identification of handwriting, if the witness has sufficient familiarity with that handwriting, is a good example of proper lay witness opinion. Here, it is not necessary that the witness be qualified as an expert, so answer B is incorrect. Answer C is incorrect because the witness who testifies as to the handwriting must be familiar with it. Answer D is incorrect because even though a witness can still testify, the witness' bias can be explored on cross-examination.

———————

12. Tom Jones and Bob Smith kidnapped a young eight year old girl who was walking to school. After being arrested, Bob Smith told the investigators that the kidnapping was Tom's idea. At trial Bob changes his story and claims that the eight year old girl begged them for a ride, and that he didn't pay attention to how Tom treated the child. The prosecution may lawfully:

A. Attack Bob's credibility with his prior inconsistent statements to the investigators.

B. Attack Bob's credibility since he was not in a position to observe the events.

C. Not attack Bob's credibility since he is testifying under oath during the trial.

D. Not attack Bob's credibility since he is obviously confused about the events.

Correct Answer: A. A witness can be impeached by his prior inconsistent statements. B is incorrect because Bob has already given statements that showed he observed the events. C is incorrect because Bob can be impeached by prior inconsistent statements. D is incorrect because Bob can be impeached based upon his previous statements. A witness can also be impeached on the fact he is confused about the events to which he is testifying.

———————

13. Fred Smith is the defendant in a trial for shoplifting. 6 years ago, Fred received a felony conviction for theft. Is this conviction admissible against Fred during the case in chief (the case on the merits)?

A. Yes, because whether Fred testifies or not, the conviction is admissible to show that Fred is a thief.

B. If Fred testifies, the prior conviction is admissible to impeach Fred.

C. No, because convictions are admissible to impeach any witness except a defendant.

D. Even if Fred testifies, the prior conviction is inadmissible because it is not relevant.

Correct Answer: B. One cannot use uncharged misconduct to show "the defendant did it before so he did it again." This rule makes A an incorrect answer. If a witness - to include a defendant- testifies, they may be impeached to lessen their credibility (believability) in the eyes of the jury. One form of impeachment is a felony conviction that is 10 years old or less or any conviction for perjury or crimes of falsity. The type of offense for which a defendant was convicted does NOT have to be similar to the type of offense that is being tried; remember that "propensity" is not a basis for admissibility. Prior convictions are admissible to impeach because the fact that a person has been convicted of a felony, or making false statements, is a matter the jury may consider in deciding whether to believe the witness. For these reasons, B is the correct answer. C is incorrect because any witness who testifies, to include the defendant, can be impeached with a prior conviction that meets the criteria mentioned above. D is incorrect because evidence that may attack a witness' credibility is relevant. Remember that arrests without a conviction, and juvenile adjudications, are not "convictions" for purposes of impeachment.

———————

14. Timmy Smith, a prominent local businessman, is on trial for kidnapping and raping two young girls from his neighborhood who were only ten years old. Timmy Smith owns a pest control business and has faithfully donated over one million dollars to the local church he has attended for the past five years. During his trial, the preacher of his church testifies that he has known the defendant for over ten years, and that he is not the type of man that would ever harm a child. What about the preacher's testimony might be a basis for impeachment?

A. The defendant has donated to the church.

B. The preacher and the defendant are friends.

C. The defendant is on trial for stealing.

D. Both A and B.

Correct Answer: D. A witness may be biased for or against another witness or an issue in trial because the witness with a bias may tend to color or slant their testimony. Bias can arise when witnesses are members of similar groups such as attending the same church. Also, in this example, the defendant has contributed financially to the preacher's church. The preacher's credibility could be attacked based upon his bias towards the defendant.

———————

15. You and your partner investigated Sam Criminal for 2 years. Your partner compiled a lengthy investigative report. You did not make a report. You testify for the government at Sam Criminal's trial. During direct-examination you are asked the name of Sam Criminal's wife. At that moment, you can't remember her name. However, you do remember that the name of Sam Criminal's wife is in your partner's investigative report, and that the AUSA brought that report to the trial. Can your partner's investigative report be used to refresh your memory?

A. No, because the information in the report is about Sam Criminal's wife, not the person on trial.

B. No, because it was prepared by your partner, and not you.

C. Yes, but only if your partner took an oath that the report is true.

D. Yes, because anything can be used to refresh your recollection.

Correct Answer: D. Anything can be used to refresh recollection, regardless of whether it was prepared by the witness or not. A is incorrect because a witness may refresh their recollection regarding any subject on which they are questioned at trial. B is incorrect because it is acceptable to use your partner's report to refresh your memory even if you did not prepare the report. C is incorrect because anything can be used to refresh a witness' recollection. If a document is used it does not have to have been made under oath.

———————

16. Anna Smith is the mother of a child victim who was kidnapped and murdered five blocks from the family's residence. During the trial of her child's killer, Ms. Smith is asked to give the approximate date and time she first noticed her child missing. She can not remember, but the investigator has a copy of her phone records showing when the mother of the victim first called the police. Can the phone records be used to refresh Ms. Smith's memory?

A. No, the phone records were not made under oath.

B. No, a witness can only use notes or documents he or she prepared to refresh memory

C. Yes, because the jury will have the phone records in evidence anyway.

D. Yes, because a witness can use any document to refresh memory, regardless of whether or not the witness prepared it.

Correct Answer: D. If a witness forgets a fact while testifying, their memory can be "refreshed." The rule is that "anything can be used to refresh a witness' memory." Sketches, photos, physical objects, reports, notes, and even "unofficial items" such as documents prepared by other LEOs or non-LEOs can be used. Documents or statements used to refresh memory do not have to be under oath. When a witness' memory is refreshed, the witness can then testify from memory. Answer A is wrong, because there is no requirement that the documents be made under oath. Answer B is wrong, because anything can be used to refresh a witness' memory including the notes or documents of others. Answer C is wrong, because the report or record used to refresh memory is neither read nor given to the jury as the witness will be testifying from their refreshed memory. The phone records will not be submitted as evidence, but rather will be used by the witness to refresh memory.

Students should note that while a document used to refresh memory will not be given to the jury, it will be shown to the defense counsel. The defense counsel can use other information in the document during cross-examination.

Courtroom Evidence Practice Exam

17. In order to use your notes during testimony to refresh your recollection, which is true regarding when the jury sees your notes?

A. The jury must have received your notes at the start of the trial before you can use them.

B. The jury must be given a copy of your notes immediately following your testimony.

C. The jury must be given a copy of your notes before the conclusion of the evidence.

D. It is irrelevant whether the jury ever sees a copy of your notes.

Correct Answer: D. Using notes to refresh recollection has nothing to do with whether the jury ever sees the notes. A copy of the notes may be offered into evidence for some other reason, but they will not be provided to the jury when they are only used to refresh witness recollection.

———————

18. You arrest Sam for fraud. After Sam waives his Miranda rights, Sam tells you, "Yes, I scammed that little old lady for all her life savings." At trial and during the government's case in chief, you are asked to tell the jury what Sam told you during the interview. The defense objects claiming the statement is hearsay. Is the statement admissible?

A. No, because the statement is hearsay.

B. No, because the government is required to call the defendant to testify in the matter.

C. Yes, because the statement is not hearsay.

D. Yes, because the statement is hearsay but subject to an exception.

Correct Answer: C. Statements and admissions of the defendant that are offered by the prosecution are excluded from the definition of hearsay. So, if a defendant makes an out of court statement that is offered in court, that statement is admissible and no exception is necessary. Statements and admissions of a defendant are not hearsay because the government is unable to call the defendant to the stand to have the maker of the statement testify. (On the other hand, if the defense offers the statement of the defendant, it is hearsay – because the defense can call the defendant to the stand.) Answer A is incorrect because, as stated above, the defendant's statement is not hearsay. We hope you said B is incorrect; the government can NEVER call the defendant to the stand during a trial. D is incorrect because the defendant's statement is not, by definition, hearsay and therefore an exception is not necessary.

———————

19. You are a uniformed officer on patrol and are called to a violent, domestic disturbance. When you arrive at the scene, you see a man and woman arguing. Suddenly, the woman appears to lunge at the man, stab the man with a shiny object, and then flees. As soon as the woman made the stabbing motion, the man jumps back and exclaims, "I can't believe she cut me!" You learn that the man and woman are not married. When the ambulance arrives, an EMT asks, "How did you get this cut?" The man replies, "I got stabbed with a knife." A knife is never found. After the woman is indicted, you learn that, unfortunately, the man is killed in an auto accident and obviously will not be able to testify at the trial. At the woman's trial for assault with a dangerous weapon, the prosecution offers the statement the victim made when stabbed and the statement to the EMT. Are these statements admissible?

A. Both statements are admissible because reliable witnesses can testify they were in fact made.

B. Both statements are admissible because, though hearsay, there are exceptions that apply.

C. Neither statement is admissible because they are both hearsay and no exceptions apply.

D. The statement when being stabbed is admissible, but the statement to the EMT is not because the EMT is not a physician.

Correct Answer B. The hearsay rule states that if (1) a statement is made out of court and that statement is (2) offered in court and (3) the statement is offered for the truth of the matter asserted, then the statement is hearsay. Hearsay is inadmissible in court unless there is an exception. Here, the prosecutor wants the jury to hear the two statements that the victim made, and furthermore, wants the jury to believe the statements are true (that the victim was cut, and that he was cut with a knife.) Both of the statements are hearsay. The excited utterance exception applies to the statement about being cut. The law recognizes that statements made under emotional stress are unlikely to be fabricated. The excited utterance exception applies when: (a) the person making the statement experienced a startling event, (b) the statement was made while the person was under the stress or excitement caused by the event, and (c) the statement was about the startling event. The medical treatment exception applies to the statement made to the EMT. That exception applies when a person is speaking to health care providers about why they are sick or injured. The law recognizes that during such circumstances a person is unlikely to fabricate. The elements of this exception are: (a) a statement is made for the purposes of medical diagnosis or treatment, (b) the statement concerns medical history, past or present symptoms, pain, sensations, or the cause of the medical problem, and (c) the statement is pertinent to the diagnosis or treatment. If the person making the statement believes that the person they are speaking to is someone who is going to help them medically, the statement can qualify under this exception. The statement need not be made to a physician, but just someone from whom the speaker expects to receive medical treatment or diagnosis, including nurses, EMTs, or physicians. A is incorrect because it doesn't matter that a reliable witness can testify to the statement; the statement is still hearsay. C is incorrect because though the statements are hearsay, exceptions apply to both statements. D is incorrect because, as previously discussed, both statements though hearsay, have exceptions. Students should remember that there are many other hearsay exceptions that are outside FLETC training, and your AUSA will know of them. The officer's job is to document the facts and circumstances surrounding the making of any statements so if the prosecutor needs to use a hearsay exception, he or she will have the facts to do so.

———————

20. In preparing for trial, the AUSA learns that the defendant is going to claim an alibi defense at trial saying he was not in town when the crime occurred. Your investigation revealed the defendant was in fact staying at Motel 6 in town at the time of the crime. You track down Francis, who is head registration clerk at the Motel 6, and she finds the registration for the defendant showing he stayed at the hotel the night of the crime. Francis doesn't have any personal knowledge of the transaction because she wasn't the clerk that night, Edward was. Francis can say that the registration form was prepared at the time of registration and has been kept in the cabinet all along. She signs an attesting certificate as a custodian to that fact. When the registration form and the certificate are offered in evidence, the defense objects for a lack of authentication. Is the form and certificate admissible?

A. No, because the government needs a witness with personal knowledge-Edward- to authenticate the document.

B. No, because a foundation can be laid by only a law enforcement officer.

C. Yes, because the authentication requirement does not apply to documents that have signatures.

D. Yes, because the AUSA can properly authenticate the documents.

Correct Answer D: The AUSA can properly authenticate the documents. Business records can be admitted as evidence as long as there is an attesting certificate signed by the custodian that: (1) the record was made at or near the time to which the record pertains by a person with knowledge of the matter, (2) the record was kept in the ordinary course of business, and (3) the business made such a record as a regular practice. There is no requirement that the custodian of records have made the entries in the record, and no requirement that Edward authenticate the document. The AUSA can lay a proper foundation (self-authentication) to have the documents admitted as business records if he has an attesting certificate described above. Answer A is incorrect because it is not necessary to have Edward testify about the records to have them properly authenticated. The Federal Rules of Evidence permits authentication of these records when accompanied by an attesting certificate signed by a custodian. The custodian of the records, Francis has prepared an attesting certificate as a custodian of the records. This is sufficient. B is incorrect because it is not necessary to have the testimony of a law enforcement officer to properly authenticate the evidence. C is incorrect, because the authentication requirement does apply to documents that have signatures.

21. Bobby Bazooka is being tried for federal firearms violations and has been previously convicted for the felony crime of armed robbery in Glynn County Superior Court. One of the charges pending against Bazooka in the criminal indictment is possession of a firearm by a convicted felon. The prosecutor seeks to have a certified copy of Bazooka's prior conviction for armed robbery admitted as evidence during the trial. Bazooka's defense attorney objects that the copy of the conviction has not been authenticated. The judge should:

A. Not admit the certified copy of Bazooka's prior criminal conviction since it is clearly inadmissible hearsay.

B. Not admit Bazooka's certified copy of prior criminal conviction since it is not relevant on the issues being tried in the case.

C. Admit the certified copy of prior criminal conviction only if the original criminal indictment, guilty plea, and sentence are tendered as the best evidence.

D. Admit Bazooka's certified copy of prior criminal conviction as a public record.

Correct Answer: D. The Federal Rules of Evidence permit public records and documents to be self-authenticating if they are accompanied by a seal or certified as correct by the custodian. Since the copy of the prior criminal conviction is certified by the clerk's office, it could be properly admitted as a public record. There is no requirement that the original indictment, plea, and sentence be offered as evidence. A certified copy will suffice as a public record. The certified copy of conviction certainly has a direct bearing on the issue being tried, that is, possession of a firearm by a convicted felon. The prosecution has the burden to prove beyond a reasonable doubt that the defendant is a convicted felon in order to convict the defendant.

---

22. The Best Evidence rule requires that:

A. A fact must have a tendency to prove or disprove a fact in issue to be admissible at trial.

B. A fact is not admissible in trial unless the person offering the fact can prove it is the best evidence of that fact.

C. A fact must prove something in issue directly, and not indirectly.

D. To prove the contents of a writing, the original of that writing must be used if available.

Correct Answer: D. The Best Evidence Rule is best remembered as "the original document rule." This rule requires that if a party at trial wants to prove what a document says – like a letter, cancelled check, or a contract – the original of that document must be used. So, if in a fraud case the AUSA wants to prove that the victim received a letter that offered gold at $25 per ounce, the AUSA would have to prove that with the use of the letter. (There are exceptions to the Best Evidence Rule that are beyond the scope of agent/officer training.) A is incorrect because that answer is the definition of relevance. B is incorrect because there is no such rule. C is incorrect because both direct and indirect (circumstantial) evidence is admissible.

---

23. Grannie Mae, an elderly grandmother, was taken advantage of by some con artists operating in Florida. The criminals sold her a fraudulent bond for $15,000.00. The bond is actually a worthless piece of paper. The investigators on the mail fraud case contacted Grannie Mae in order to secure the original bond as evidence for the case. Grannie Mae insists that she will only provide the investigators with a copy of the original bond, because she wants to keep the original bond itself. The investigators obtained a copy of the worthless bond for evidence. Two weeks before the trial of the mail fraud case, the original bond burned up in Grannie Mae's house fire when she left the oven on all night. The copy of the bond is:

A. Inadmissible because the original bond is required for it to be admissible.

B. Inadmissible because the investigators should have safeguarded the original bond.

C. Admissible because the original bond itself is unavailable, and a copy will be sufficient.

D. Admissible because the best evidence rule only applies to writings not bonds.

Correct Answer: C. The Best Evidence Rule states that to prove the contents of a writing, the original writing itself must be admitted into evidence; witnesses are not permitted to testify what a document says over defense objection. If the document is available, it must be admitted into evidence. There are exceptions such as when all originals have been lost or are unobtainable, or the other side has the original and will not produce it. Duplicates include carbon copies, photocopies, or copies made from other techniques that accurately reproduce the original. Duplicates can be used when the original is lost or unobtainable. Answer A is incorrect because based on the Best Evidence Rule, if the original writing is lost or unobtainable, a copy can be used. Answer B is incorrect because even though it would be good investigative work to obtain the original bond, it is acceptable to use the copy in evidence since the original was lost in the fire. Answer D is incorrect because the Best Evidence Rule applies to any writing including bonds.

Electronic Law and Evidence Practice Exam

1. Assuming no one gives consent, which of the following would require a Title III court order?

a. Intercepting tone only pager signals using a device.

b. Using GPS and other mobile tracking devices.

c. Real time interceptions of wire communications using a device.

d. Real time interceptions of oral communications, in which there is no reasonable expectation of privacy (REP), using a device.

---

a. Intercepting tone only pager signals using a device.
Incorrect. These are explicitly excluded from the requirements of Title III.

b. Using GPS and other mobile tracking devices.
Incorrect. These are explicitly excluded from the requirements of Title III.

c. Real time interceptions of wire communications using a device.
Correct. Using a device to perform a non-consensual, real time interception of a wire communication, whether there is REP in the communication or not, requires a TIII court order.

d. Real time interceptions of oral communications, in which there is no reasonable expectation of privacy (REP), using a device.
Incorrect. Only those real-time, non-consensual interceptions, using a device, of oral communications in which there is REP require a TIII court order.

2. In which of the following situations would law enforcement officers need a Title III court order?

a. Listen in to a phone conversation among five people with the consent of only one party to the conversation.

b. Place a covert listening and recording device on a confidential informant (with his permission) to record conversations he has with the target of an investigation.

c. Conceal a microphone and transmitter in a vehicle to listen to the conversations that two targets have while in the vehicle.

d. Obtain the telephone numbers that a target is calling without the consent of the caller or the person receiving the call.

---

a. Listen in to a phone conversation among five people with the consent of only one party to the conversation.
Incorrect. If there is consent from one or more parties to the conversation and the conversation is being intercepted for law enforcement purposes, a TIII is not required.

b. Place a covert listening and recording device on a confidential informant (with his permission) to record conversations he has with the target of an investigation.
Incorrect. This is a face-to-face consensual intercept. This activity, however, would require advising the AUSA that such an intercept is being conducted.

c. Conceal a microphone and transmitter in a vehicle to listen to the conversations that two targets have while in the vehicle.
Correct. Title III is triggered here because there is a real time interception of an REP, oral communication, using a device, and without the consent of any of the parties to the conversation.

d. Obtain the telephone numbers that a target is calling without the consent of the caller or the person receiving the call.
Incorrect. This describes a pen register, and this information can be obtained with a Pen Register court order. If agents want to intercept the *contents* of the phone call, they would need a TIII court order or consent of at least one party to the conversation.

3. Agents know that Jack and Fred are members of a criminal conspiracy. To avoid their communications being intercepted by law enforcement, they only talk together when walking along trails in a local city park being careful to speak softly and avoid those that might be around who could overhear what they are saying. Agents decide to use a handheld parabolic microphone that can pick up human conversations at 250 feet without being detected. To lawfully use this device under these circumstances, what arrangements must the agents first make to comply with the law?

a. There are no special legal requirements.

b. Obtain a search warrant.

c. Request a Title III court order through the US Attorney for approval by a US Magistrate Judge.

d. Request a Title III court order through the US Attorney for approval by a US District Court judge.

_____

a. There are no special legal requirements.
Incorrect. Real-time non-consensual interceptions, using a device, of oral communications in which there is REP require a TIII court order. The conversation is one in which the parties would have both a subjective and objectively reasonable expectation of privacy.

b. Obtain a search warrant.
Incorrect. See the correct answer below.

c. Request a Title III court order through the US Attorney for approval by a US Magistrate Judge.
Incorrect. See the correct answer below.

d. Request a Title III court order through the US Attorney for approval by a US District Court judge.
Correct. The application would be submitted through the AUSA and US Attorney to the Department of Justice. If the application is approved, it would then be given to a District Court judge for approval. A US Magistrate Judge cannot act on the application.

4. Fred's criminal enterprise involves sending and receiving faxes. Assume that agents have probable cause. Which is correct concerning how agents could obtain the faxes?

a. If the fax is in the process of being transmitted, agents could use a search warrant issued by a Magistrate Judge to connect a fax machine to Fred's phone line and receive a copy of the fax as Fred gets his copy.

b. If the fax is in the process of being transmitted, agents could use a search warrant issued by a District Court judge to connect a fax machine to Fred's phone line and receive a copy of the fax as Fred gets his copy.

c. If the fax is in the process of being transmitted, and there is also REP, agents could use a search warrant issued by a District Court judge to connect a fax machine to Fred's phone line and receive a copy of the fax as Fred gets his copy.

d. If the agents have probable cause paper copies of the faxes are located in Fred's house, they could use a search warrant issued by a Magistrate Judge.

---

a. If the fax is in the process of being transmitted, agents could use a search warrant issued by a Magistrate Judge to connect a fax machine to Fred's phone line and receive a copy of the fax as Fred gets his copy.
Incorrect. This requires a Title III order because it is a real-time interception of an electronic communication using a device without consent.

b. If the fax is in the process of being transmitted, agents could use a search warrant issued by a District Court judge to connect a fax machine to Fred's phone line and receive a copy of the fax as Fred gets his copy.
Incorrect. See the justification for answer a above.

c. If the fax is in the process of being transmitted, and there is also REP, agents could use a search warrant issued by a District Court judge to connect a fax machine to Fred's phone line and receive a copy of the fax as Fred gets his copy.
Incorrect. The only difference between this answer and answer b is that there is REP. Title III applies, however, to the real time interception of wire and electronic communications whether or not there is REP. Title III applies, however, only to oral communications in which there is REP.

d. If the agents have probable cause paper copies of the faxes are located in Fred's house, they could use a search warrant issued by a Magistrate Judge.
Correct. This does not involve Title III because there is no real-time interception.

5. Investigation reveals that a gang is operating a mobile meth lab and distributing large quantities of meth to various dealers. These dealers also move from location to location. Agents decide to use GPS and other tracking devices to try and determine where the current meth lab and dealers are. Which of the following activities would require the agents to obtain a warrant? (Assume that the gang members do not know of the agents' activities.)

a. Concealing a GPS tracking device on the exterior of a target's vehicle as the vehicle sits in a public parking lot.

b. Concealing a GPS tracking device inside a box of meth production products (glassware, tubing, and the like), sending it to the target, and monitoring where the box moves along local highways and streets.

c. Concealing a GPS or radio frequency tracking device inside a small package of meth precursor chemicals, sending it to the target, and monitoring where the package goes to include inside homes and factory buildings.

d. None of the above, because the Stored Electronic Communications Act, and not 4th Amendment warrants, must be used for the installation or use of mobile tracking devices.

---

a. Concealing a GPS tracking device on the exterior of a target's vehicle as the vehicle sits in a public parking lot.
Incorrect. There is no intrusion into REP so a warrant is not required.

b. Concealing a GPS tracking device inside a box of meth production products (glassware, tubing, and the like), sending it to the target, and monitoring where the box moves along local highways and streets.
Incorrect. There is no intrusion into REP to install the device, so a warrant is not required to install. Since the box is being monitored in public places, a warrant is not required to monitor the device.

c. Concealing a GPS or radio frequency tracking device inside a small package of meth precursor chemicals, sending it to the target, and monitoring where the package goes to include inside homes and factory buildings.
Correct. A warrant is not required to install the device because there is no intrusion into REP. A warrant is required to monitor the device because the item will be tracked as it moves in REP areas.

d. None of the above, because the Stored Electronic Communications Act, and not 4th Amendment warrants, must be used for the installation or use of mobile tracking devices.
Incorrect. Mobile tracking devices are explicitly excluded from the requirements of Title III. The Stored Communications Act is not applicable to this situation.

6. Agents have reasonable suspicion that Fred uses email and the telephone in support of his criminal activity. The investigation is not at the point where agents have probable cause to get a warrant, but knowing who Fred corresponds with by way of email or speaks with on the phone would be relevant to this ongoing criminal investigation. Agents are interested in obtaining any or all of the following: the email addresses and phone numbers of those who email Fred and those that Fred calls or emails. Which of the following is correct concerning what "paper" agents must use to obtain this information?

a. No paper can get this information because agents do not have probable cause.

b. No paper is necessary to get this information because Fred has no REP in this information.

c. A Pen Register court order for the incoming phone numbers and email addresses.

d. A Trap and Trace court order for the incoming phone numbers and email addresses.

---

a. No paper can get this information because agents do not have probable cause.
Incorrect: To get a Pen register Court order or a Trap and Trace court order, the information only has to be relevant to an ongoing criminal investigation.

b. No paper is necessary to get this information because Fred has no REP in this information.
Incorrect: While the courts have ruled there is no REP in at least the phone number information, the Pen-Trap statute requires a court order.

c. A Pen Register court order for the incoming phone numbers and email addresses.
Incorrect: A Pen Register court order is used to capture the outgoing phone numbers or email addresses.

d. A Trap and Trace court order for the incoming phone numbers and email addresses.
Correct.

7. Agents need to obtain a Pen Register or Trap and Trace court order. Which of the following is correct about who makes the request to the judge, what judge can approve it, and how long the court order is good for?

a. Agent requests, Magistrate Judge can issue, good for 60 days.

b. AUSA requests, Magistrate Judge can issue, good for 60 days.

c. AUSA requests, requires at least District Court approval, good for 45 days.

d. Agent requests, Magistrate Judge can issue, good for 45 days.

---

a. Agent requests, Magistrate Judge can issue, good for 60 days.
Incorrect.

b. AUSA requests, Magistrate Judge can issue, good for 60 days.
Correct.

c. AUSA requests, requires at least District Court approval, good for 45 days.
Incorrect.

d. Agent requests, Magistrate Judge can issue, good for 45 days.
Incorrect.

8. Agents want to use video only surveillance (no audio) to determine who has been pilfering items from a commercial facility. Agents have consent from the facility owner to install the camera. Which of the below is a correct statement of the legal authority agents will need when deciding what images to capture and where they can point the camera?

a. A TIII court order is necessary if the camera captures images from an area where people have REP.

b. Neither a search warrant nor a TIII is necessary no matter where the camera is pointed.

c. Because of the intrusiveness of capturing video of private activity, a warrant is required no matter where the camera is pointed.

d. If the camera is pointed at an REP area, a warrant is required.

---

a. A TIII court order is necessary if the camera captures images from an area where people have REP.
Incorrect. TIII does not apply to the capture of video, just oral, wire, and electronic communications.

b. Neither a search warrant nor a TIII is necessary no matter where the camera is pointed.
Incorrect. See the justification to question d.

c. Because of the intrusiveness of capturing video of private activity, a warrant is required no matter where the camera is pointed.
Incorrect. See the justification to question d.

d. If the camera is pointed at an REP area, a warrant is required.
Correct. The 4th Amendment applies to the placement of video only surveillance as well as the images that will be captured. If access to REP is required to install the camera, a warrant or 4th Amendment exception is required. A warrant or an 4th Amendment exception is also required if the camera captures images in a place in which one has REP.

9. Note to students. You will not see a test question from the legal division in below format. The below format is only to make this practice exam more efficient.

Agents want the data listed in column A from the Internet Service Provider. The subscriber will not be asked for consent. Write in Column B what type of "paper" they need. If more than one type of paper will work, write in the one that is legally the easiest to get.

A. What you want	Possible answers (The same answer may be used more than once.)	B. What you need
Email addresses of email correspondents (not contents)		
Web browsing history (transactional record)		
Unopened emails that have been in electronic storage for less than 180 days	a. No paper. b. Subpoena. c. 2703(d) court order. d. Search warrant. e. Title III court order.	
Name of customer and method of payment (basic subscriber information)		
Unopened emails that have been in electronic storage for 180 days or more.		
Opened emails in electronic storage.		

A. What you want	Possible answers (The same answer may be used more than once.)	B. What you need
Email addresses of email correspondents (not contents)		C
Web browsing history (transactional record)		C
Unopened emails that have been in electronic storage for less than 180 days	a. No paper. b. Subpoena. c. 2703(d) court order. d. Search warrant. e. Title III court order.	D
Name of customer and method of payment (basic subscriber information)		B
Unopened emails that have been in electronic storage for 180 days or more.		B
Opened emails in electronic storage.		B

10. Agents have probable cause that Jack runs a stolen credit card ring from his home computer in District A, and that others who are part of the ring buy and sell stolen credit cards in Districts B, and C. Agents develop probable cause that there is evidence that Jack has data stored on a web server located in District D. In addition, there is probable cause that Jack's Internet Service provider in District D has unopened emails to Jack that have been in electronic storage for less than 90 days. Agents want all the evidence (emails and data), and they decide to use search warrants. Which statement is correct concerning which District the agents may lawfully obtain a warrant?

a. For all the information (data and emails), they can obtain a warrant only in District A.

b. For the data, they can obtain a warrant in Districts A, B, C or D.

c. For the emails, they can obtain a warrant in Districts A, B, C or D.

d. For the emails, they can obtain a warrant only in the District D.

---

a. For all the information (data and emails), they can obtain a warrant only in District A.
Incorrect. See the explanation at the bottom of this page.

b. For the data, they can obtain a warrant in Districts A, B, C or D.
Incorrect. See the explanation at the bottom of this page.

c. For the emails, they can obtain a warrant in Districts A, B, C or D.
Correct. See the explanation at the bottom of this page.

d. For the emails, they can obtain a warrant only in the District D.
Incorrect. See the explanation at the bottom of this page.

Explanation.
For data, they can obtain a warrant ONLY in the District in which the data is located.

To obtain the stored electronic communications (emails), they can obtain a warrant from any federal judge with jurisdiction over the offense under investigation; this warrant is valid in any jurisdiction where the stored emails may be. Since aspects of this criminal ring operates in Districts A, B, C and D, agents may obtain a search warrant for the stored emails in any of those districts; this warrant will be valid in any other district.

11. Fred is lawfully arrested. He has a pager on his person. Can agents search this pager without a warrant?

a. Yes, because having a pager on one's person when being arrested is consent to have it searched.

b. Yes, because searching the pager is within the scope of an SIA.

c. No, because the pager may contain wire or electronic communications and that requires a Title III court order.

d. No, because it is unreasonable to search without a warrant or Title III court order.

---

a. Yes, because having a pager on one's person when being arrested is consent to have it searched.
Incorrect. Consent must be knowingly and voluntarily given to be valid.

b. Yes, because searching the pager is within the scope of an SIA.
Correct.

c. No, because the pager may contain wire or electronic communications and that requires a Title III court order.
Incorrect. While the pager might contain such communications, searching them would not involve intercepting a *real-time* interception.

d. No, because it is unreasonable to search without a warrant or Title III court order.
Incorrect. Searches incident to arrest are considered reasonable, and pagers carried by an arrestee are within the scope of an SIA.

12. Fred is at a restaurant and is using his computer. An agent can see the screen from an adjoining table and sees the screen contains an email that clearly constitutes wire fraud. As the agent walks up, Fred furiously starts deleting files. The agent seizes the computer and then immediately searches it finding evidence of wire fraud. Was the seizure and search of Fred's computer lawful?

a. Both the seizure and the search were lawful.

b. Neither the seizure nor the search were lawful.

c. The seizure was lawful; the search was not.

d. The seizure was unlawful; the search was lawful.

---

a. Both the seizure and the search were lawful.
Incorrect. See the justification to the correct answer.

b. Neither the seizure nor the search were lawful.
Incorrect. See the justification to the correct answer.

c. The seizure was lawful; the search was not.
Correct. The seizure was lawful because of the exigency that if the computer was not immediately seized, evidence of crime would be destroyed before a warrant could be obtained. Once this exigency ended with the computer's seizure, the ability to lawfully use this 4th Amendment exception ended.

d. The seizure was unlawful; the search was lawful.
Incorrect. See the justification to the correct answer.

13. Agent Jones has a valid search warrant to search Fred's computer hard drive for evidence of wire fraud. During and within the scope of the types of data the warrant authorizes a search for, Fred sees what is clearly evidence of larceny of government property (unrelated to the wire fraud crimes). Fred continues the search for wire fraud and sees more evidence of larceny. He seizes this evidence of the larceny. Was the evidence of the larceny lawfully seized?

a. ALL the evidence of the larceny was lawfully seized.

b. NONE of the evidence of the larceny was lawfully seized.

c. The first evidence of the larceny Fred saw was lawfully seized; the second and subsequent seizures were not.

d. The second and subsequent seizures of the larceny evidence were lawfully seized only if Fred first got another warrant before continuing his search after he first saw the evidence of the larceny.

---

a. ALL the evidence of the larceny was lawfully seized.
Correct. Fred stayed within the scope of the warrant, and so the larceny evidence he saw was lawfully seized under the plain view doctrine.

b. NONE of the evidence of the larceny was lawfully seized.
Incorrect. See the justification above.

c. The first evidence of the larceny Fred saw was lawfully seized; the second and subsequent seizures were not.
Incorrect. See the justification to answer a.

d. The second and subsequent seizures of the larceny evidence were lawfully seized only if Fred first got another warrant before continuing his search after he first saw the evidence of the larceny.
Incorrect. See the justification to answer a.

More information to consider.
1. If a court found that Fred abandoned his search for evidence of the wire fraud and began to look for evidence of the larceny – or just began to look specifically for evidence of the larceny – a court could likely find that only the first evidence of the larceny would be admissible. This is so because Fred would be outside the scope of the warrant (evidence of wire fraud) and was therefore not "lawfully present" when he saw the evidence of the larceny. "Lawfully present" is a prerequisite to make a lawful seizure under plain view.

2. Whenever evidence of a crime outside the scope of the warrant is seen, the best practice is to stop the search, and request a warrant (sometimes called a 'secondary" or "piggy-back" warrant) to search for the newly discovered evidence.

14. What is the most significant difference in preparing a search warrant to search computers for data and a search warrant for physical items?

A data warrant:

a. Does not have to particularly describe what is to be searched for.

b. Does not have to particularly describe the place or thing to be searched.

c. Does not require probable cause.

d. Must include a justification if agents want to conduct an off-site search.

A data warrant:

a. Does not have to particularly describe what is to be searched for.
Incorrect. This is required by the 4th Amendment.

b. Does not have to particularly describe the place or thing to be searched.
Incorrect. This is required by the 4th Amendment.

c. Does not require probable cause.
Incorrect. This is required by the 4th Amendment.

d. Must include a justification if agents want to conduct an off-site search.
Correct.

15. Agents ask consent to search Fred's computer. Fred gives consent. When agents go to search the computer, they see a CD labeled, "Child Porn collection 1" sitting by the keyboard. The CD is seized and is immediately searched. Was Fred's consent legally sufficient to search the CD?

a. Yes, because a CD is something that can be read only with a computer.

b. Yes, because a CD is a computer component.

c. No, because the scope of consent did not include media not in the computer.

d. No, because consent is not a valid basis to search for data.

_____

a. Yes, because a CD is something that can be read only with a computer.
Incorrect. See the justification for the correct answer.

b. Yes, because a CD is a computer component.
Incorrect. A CD is not a computer component. See also the justification for the correct answer.

c. No, because the scope of consent did not include media not in the computer.
Correct. A CD is not a computer, and that is all that Fred gave consent to search. If agents had asked to search for "evidence of crime" or to search "the computer and media," the consent would have extended to the CD. The seizure of the CD was valid because agents had probable cause it contained evidence of a crime, and it is reasonable to preserve the evidence from immediate destruction. But once the CD was seized, the exigency to search the CD can no longer be supported by the exigent circumstances exception.

d. No, because consent is not a valid basis to search for data.
Incorrect. Consent can be a valid basis to search.

16. What is the applicability of the knock and announce statute (18 U.S.C. Section 3109) to the execution of search warrants of computers or for data?

a. The statute is not applicable.

b. The statute is applicable, but the exceptions are not.

c. The statute and its exceptions are both applicable.

d. While the statute and its exceptions may be applicable, exceptions do not arise in searches of computers or for data.

_____

a. The statute is not applicable.
Incorrect.

b. The statute is applicable, but the exceptions are not.
Incorrect. Both the statute and its exceptions are applicable.

c. The statute and its exceptions are both applicable.
Correct.

d. While the statute and its exceptions may be applicable, exceptions do not arise in searches of computers or for data.
Incorrect. Both the statute and its exceptions are applicable. Data is easily destructible which can be the basis of an exception. Those who have computers or data that is evidence of a crime can present a danger to officers which can also be the basis of a knock and announce exception.

17. Which is a correct statement with respect to authenticating (laying a foundation for) computer or electronic data that is admitted into court?

a. Laying a foundation and authentication are not required.

b. While preventing data from being altered once it has been seized is important, once data is seized there is no need to prove who authored, possessed, and had the data in order to secure a conviction.

c. Circumstantial evidence, such as access to computers or data, fingerprints, and passwords, is valuable to prove who may have generated or had access to data.

d. The rules of evidence do not apply to trials that involve criminal possession of data.

_____

a. Laying a foundation and authentication are not required.
Incorrect: These requirements must be met.

b. While preventing data from being altered once it has been seized is important, once data is seized there is no need to prove who authored, possessed, and had the data in order to secure a conviction.
Incorrect: Even if data is admitted, it must still be connected to a particular person in order to be relevant.

c. Circumstantial evidence, such as access to computers or data, fingerprints, and passwords, is valuable to prove who may have generated or had access to data.
Correct: For example, in cases where data is found on a public computer or one to which many had access, circumstantial evidence is invaluable to connect the data to a particular person.

d. The rules of evidence do not apply to trials that involve criminal possession of data.
Incorrect: The rules of evidence apply in all criminal trials regardless of the offense being prosecuted.

Federal Court Procedures Practice Exam

1. Al is convicted of drug trafficking in U.S. District Court. Where would he appeal this conviction?

A. Supreme Court

B. Circuit Court

C. State Court

D. He has no right to appeal.

Answer: B. The Circuit Court of Appeals hears all appeals from convictions in District Court. If the Supreme Court did consider this case, it would not do so until *after* the Circuit Court made a decision. The state court systems do not consider appeals of federal cases.

_____

2. Dan Defendant has been arrested for felony drug trafficking. Where will his trial be held?

A. Magistrate Court

B. District Court

C. Circuit Court

D. Supreme Court

Answer: B. The District Court presides over felony trials. The Magistrate Court judge can conduct many non-trial proceedings in a felony trial, but he cannot preside over a felony trial itself. The Circuit Court and Supreme Court could only consider appeals from this case.

_____

3. Smith is charged with a serious misdemeanor for which he could be sentenced to up to one year in prison if found guilty. Where will his trial be held?

A. It must be held in the District Court.

B. It must be held in the Magistrate Court.

C. It must be held in the Circuit Court.

D. It can be held in either the District Court or the Magistrate Court, depending on Smith.

Answer: D. The Magistrate Court can preside over any misdemeanor trial. However, for a Class A misdemeanor, (anything beyond a "petty offense," meaning any offense for which the defendant could be sentenced to imprisonment for more than 6 months but up to one year), the defendant has the right to insist on trial in the District Court. If the defendant waives his right to be tried in District Court, the trial will be held in Magistrate's Court.

———————————

4. Special Agent Smith has probable cause that Joe Criminal purchased a small amount of marijuana. Rather than arrest Criminal, Agent Smith would like Joe Criminal ordered to come into court on his own to answer to the charges. Agent Smith would have Joe Criminal served with:

A. an arrest warrant

B. a subpoena ad testificandum

C. a subpoena duces tecum

D. a summons

Answer: D. A summons directs a person to appear in court at a specific time and place regarding the crime charged in the summons. An arrest warrant commands an officer to make an arrest. A subpoena requires the appearance of a witness.

———————————

Federal Court Procedures Practice Exam

5. Special Agent Smith has concluded his investigation of Joe Criminal for drug trafficking. Agent Smith explains his case to the AUSA. The AUSA accepts the case and obtains an indictment from the Grand Jury. Agent Smith obtains an arrest warrant and arrests Joe Criminal. When must Agent Smith prepare the criminal complaint?

A. never

B. prior to indictment

C. prior to arrest

D. after arrest

Answer: A. A criminal complaint can be used to establish probable cause in support of a warrantless arrest. A criminal complaint can also be used to obtain an arrest warrant. However, when an indictment is used to obtain an arrest warrant, there is no need for a criminal complaint.

---

6. Special Agent Smith made a warrantless arrest of Joe Criminal for drug trafficking. When must Agent Smith prepare the criminal complaint?

A. never

B. after arrest, but before the Initial Appearance

C. prior to arrest, but after receiving approval by the AUSA

D. after Indictment, but before the Preliminary Hearing

Answer: B. The criminal complaint is used to establish probable cause in support of the warrantless arrest at the Initial Appearance.

Federal Court Procedures Practice Exam

7. Joe Criminal is arrested and taken to his Initial Appearance. What will happen there?

A. The Magistrate Judge will explain to the defendant the criminal charges and his rights.

B. The Grand Jury will determine if there is probable cause Joe Criminal committed the crime charged.

C. The defense attorney will present evidence of defendant's innocence.

D. The AUSA will explain to the defendant the criminal charges and his rights.

Answer: A. The Magistrate Judge will explain the charges to the defendant and advise the defendant of his rights. Evidence is not presented at an initial appearance.

---

8. Smith is arrested following indictment for drug trafficking. Pending his trial, will he be held in custody by the government?

A. No, the government has no Constitutional right to incarcerate someone who has not been found guilty.

B. Yes, following a felony arrest the defendant must remain in custody until found not guilty.

C. Smith may be released pre-trial, if Smith can demonstrate that an electronic monitoring device is sufficient to guarantee he will not leave his home.

D. Smith must be released pre-trial, unless the government establishes he is a danger to the community or a flight risk.

Answer: D. Defendants must be released pending trial unless the government demonstrates they are a flight risk or a danger to the community. Many facts can be considered in this determination, including: the seriousness of the charged offense, the defendant's ties to the local community, and the defendant's past criminal record.

Federal Court Procedures Practice Exam

9. Federal Agent Johnson just arrested Carl Criminal based on a warrant for drug trafficking. Procedurally, should he:

A. Complete booking procedures, then take Criminal to his Initial Appearance when directed by the Magistrate.

B. Take Criminal to his Initial Appearance when directed by the Magistrate, then complete booking procedures.

C. Complete booking procedures, but the Initial Appearance is not required since Criminal was arrested on a warrant.

D. Take Criminal to the Initial Appearance when directed by the Magistrate, but booking procedures are unnecessary since Criminal was arrested on a warrant.

Answer: A. Whenever someone is arrested, they will be processed by the officer through the routine booking process. This would include fingerprinting, photographing, and taking basic biographical information from the suspect. The defendant would then go to the Magistrate Judge for his Initial Appearance without unnecessary delay, whether or not he was arrested pursuant to a warrant.

———————————

10. Joe Citizen goes to visit Congressman Johnson at Johnson's office on Capitol Hill. Citizen criticizes Congressman Johnson so much that Johnson loses his temper and starts beating Joe Citizen. Federal law enforcement officers are called to the scene. These officers:

A. could not arrest Congressman Johnson because Members of Congress are immune from arrest

B. could not arrest Congressman Johnson because he is in his office on Capitol Hill

C. could arrest Congressman Johnson because he has committed a crime other than a non-violent misdemeanor

D. could not arrest Congressman Johnson, but they could detain him until impeachment proceedings begin

Answer: C. Congressman are not immune from prosecution. They are subject to felony arrest like any other person. However, they cannot be arrested for a non-violent misdemeanor while working as Congressman or traveling to or from work as a Congressman. They could be issued a citation.

———————————

Federal Court Procedures Practice Exam

11. Congressman Johnson is walking from his Capitol Hill office to the Capitol Building to attend a session of Congress. He intentionally throws some trash down on the street, committing the misdemeanor offense of littering. Federal law enforcement Officer Smith observes this misdemeanor being committed. Officer Smith:

A. could not arrest Congressman Johnson because Members of Congress can never be arrested

B. could not arrest Congressman Johnson because Congress is in session

C. could arrest Congressman Johnson because Members of Congress have no special privilege from being arrested

D. could not arrest Congressman Johnson, but could detain him until impeachment proceedings begin

Answer: B. Congressman are not immune from prosecution. They are subject to felony arrest like any other person. However, they cannot be arrested for a non-violent misdemeanor while working as Congressman or traveling to or from work as a Congressman. They could be issued a citation.

---

12. Joe Criminal robbed a bank in Brunswick, Georgia. Brunswick is in the Southern District of Georgia. Special Agent Smith arrested Joe Criminal in Macon, Georgia. Macon is in the Middle District of Georgia, adjacent to the Southern District of Georgia.

Where could Special Agent Smith take Joe Criminal for his initial appearance?

A. the Middle District of Georgia

B. the Southern District of Georgia if the Initial Appearance could be held on the day of arrest

C. either A or B

D. any Federal court with jurisdiction over Joe Criminal's offense

Answer: C. The initial appearance may always be held in the District of arrest. However, if the arrest is made in a District adjacent to the one in which the crime occurred, the defendant may be taken to that District for his Initial Appearance if the Initial Appearance can be held on the day of arrest.

Federal Court Procedures Practice Exam

13. After being indicted, Joe Criminal was arrested for drug trafficking. When will his Preliminary Hearing be held?

A. as soon as possible following the arrest

B. after the Initial Appearance, but before the Arraignment

C. after Arraignment, but prior to trial

D. never

Answer: D. If an individual has been indicted or charged by information, they will not have a Preliminary Hearing.

----

14. What happens at the Preliminary Hearing?

A. The Grand Jury decides if there is probable cause for the case to continue.

B. The Magistrate Judge decides if there is probable cause for the case to continue.

C. The Defendant must prove there is no probable cause for the case to continue.

D. The Defendant must enter a plea.

Answer: B. The Preliminary Hearing is an adversarial proceeding before the Magistrate Judge. At the Preliminary Hearing, the government has the burden of proving that there is probable cause the case should continue.

Federal Court Procedures Practice Exam

15. What happens at the Arraignment?

A. The Grand Jury decides if there is probable cause for the case to continue.

B. The Magistrate Judge decides if there is probable cause for the case to continue.

C. The Defendant must prove there is no probable cause for the case to continue.

D. The Defendant enters a plea.

Answer: D. The primary purpose of the Arraignment is for the Defendant to enter a plea.

---

16. The Grand Jury decides:

A. if probable cause exists to issue an Indictment

B. if probable cause exists to issue an Information

C. if Defendant is guilty or not guilty

D. if a Preliminary Hearing is necessary

Answer: A. If the Grand Jury determines there is probable cause the Defendant committed the charged offense, it will issue an Indictment. This is called a "true bill." If the Grand Jury did not find probable cause, it would be a "no bill."

---

17. Special Agent Johnson is investigating Joe Criminal for illegal drug activity. As part of this investigation, Agent Johnson attempted to interview Willy Witness. Willy Witness appears to have information regarding Joe Criminal's illegal activity, but is unwilling to voluntarily answer Agent Johnson's questions. Regarding Willy Witness, Agent Johnson should:

A. make no further effort since no one can make Willy Witness talk

B. offer Willy Witness money or other things of value to encourage him to cooperate

C. arrest Willy Witness for obstruction of justice

D. arrange with the AUSA to have Willy Witness subpoenaed to testify before the Grand Jury

Answer: D. Requiring an individual to appear before the Grand Jury is how the government can make uncooperative witnesses provide information. The government should not simply give up on this witness, nor should it offer him a bribe for his testimony. The mere refusal of this witness to answer questions when approached by a law enforcement officer does not constitute obstruction of justice.

———————————

18. You are a Federal law enforcement officer and want Willy Witness to appear before the Grand Jury and testify. Who do you see about getting a Grand Jury subpoena?

A. the Judge

B. the Grand Jury foreperson

C. the Court Reporter

D. the Assistant U.S. Attorney

Answer: D. The Assistant U.S. Attorney is the person who will issue subpoenas to appear before the Grand Jury.

19. You want Willy Witness to appear before the Grand Jury and testify. Willy Witness should be served with a:

A. summons testificandum

B. testimonial warrant

C. subpoena duces tecum

D. subpoena ad testificandum

Answer: D. The subpoena ad testificandum orders a person to appear and testify.

----

20. You are a Federal law enforcement agent investigating Carl Criminal. During your investigation, you witness Carl Criminal sell drugs on the street corner to a 12 year old girl. You then testify before the Grand Jury about this observation. Which of the following information could you tell your friends who are not involved in the investigation of Carl Criminal?

A. You could only tell them about witnessing the drug transaction.

B. You could tell them about witnessing the drug transaction, and that you testified before the Grand Jury. However, you could not tell them what you told the Grand Jury.

C. You could tell them about witnessing the drug transaction, and testifying before the Grand Jury, including the substance of your testimony before the Grand Jury.

D. You couldn't tell them anything about this case.

Answer: A. The witnessing of the drug transaction is not a "grand jury matter" and therefore, not secret under the grand jury secrecy rules. Accordingly, this information could be shared with others. However, the Grand Jury secrecy rules forbid the law enforcement officer from discussing the substance of his testimony before the Grand Jury. They also prevent him from stating he testified as a witness before the Grand Jury investigating Carl Criminal.

Federal Court Procedures Practice Exam

21. The AUSA learned much information from Willy Witness when Witness testified before the Grand Jury. The AUSA has shared this information with you, the Federal LEO. Who may you discuss this information with?

A. no one

B. only Federal law enforcement officers on the 6(e) list

C. any government personnel on the 6(e) list

D. anyone

Answer: C. Rule 6(e) of the Rules of Criminal Procedure authorizes disclosure of Grand Jury information to any government personnel the government attorney deems necessary to assist with the criminal investigation. These personnel should be listed on the 6(e) list maintained by the government attorney.

_____

22. Who is present when the Grand Jury is voting on whether there is probable cause to issue an Indictment?

A. only the Grand Jurors

B. only the AUSA and the Grand Jurors

C. only the court reporter and the Grand Jurors

D. only the AUSA, the Grand Jurors and the court reporter

Answer: A. Only the Grand Jurors may be present when the Grand Jury is deliberating and voting.

_____

Federal Court Procedures Practice Exam

23. Who is present when the Grand Jury is listening to witness testimony?

A. only the Grand Jurors and the witness

B. only the AUSA, the Grand Jurors and the witness

C. only the court reporter, the Grand Jurors, and the witness

D. only the AUSA, the Grand Jurors, the court reporter, and the witness

Answer: D. These are the people present when a witness is testifying before a Grand Jury.

_____

24. What document is usually used to charge a felony?

A. indictment

B. information

C. subpoena

D. bill of particulars

Answer: A. An indictment is the usual charging document in a felony case. An information, which is signed by the U.S. Attorney, may be used to charge a felony if it is a non-capital case and the defendant waives his right to indictment.

_____

25. What charging document is issued by the Grand Jury?

A. indictment

B. information

C. subpoena

D. bill of particulars

Answer: A. An indictment is the charging document issued by the Grand Jury when they find probable cause the defendant has committed the alleged offense.

_____

Federal Court Procedures Practice Exam

26. What charging document is issued by the U.S. Attorney?

A. indictment

B. information

C. subpoena

D. bill of particulars

Answer: B. An information is the charging document issued by the U.S. Attorney. It is commonly used in misdemeanor cases, and can be used in non-capital felony cases when the defendant waives his right to indictment.

---

27. Agent Smith is scheduled to be the star witness in the case against Carl Criminal. Other Agents discovered that Smith had been disciplined in the past for lying during an administrative investigation into the alleged misuse of a government vehicle. The AUSA must tell the defense attorney about this under which of the following:

A. Rule 16

B. the Brady doctrine

C. the Jencks Act

D. Giglio

Answer: D. Giglio [Giglio v. United States, 405 U.S. 150 (1974)] requires that the government give the defendant any information about government witnesses that might reasonably be used to impeach them. This includes information about prior false statements. It also includes disclosing promises made to witnesses in exchange for their testimony, such a plea bargains made in exchange for testimony.

---

28. The defense attorney has requested the AUSA provide him with a copy of defendant's criminal record. The AUSA should give him this information according to:

A. Rule 16

B. the Brady doctrine

C. the Jencks Act

D. Giglio

Answer: A. Rule 16 requires the government to provide the defendant with a copy of his criminal record if he requests it.

———————————

29. The defense attorney has requested the AUSA provide him with a copy of defendant's prior statements. The AUSA should give him these statements according to:

A. Rule 16

B. the Brady doctrine

C. the Jencks Act

D. Giglio

Answer: A. Rule 16 requires the government to provide the defendant with a copy of his prior statements (except those oral statements made to agents who the defendant did not know were agents - such as undercover agents) if he requests it.

———————————

Federal Court Procedures Practice Exam

30. Special Agent Jones is investigating Joe Criminal for bank robbery. One witness interviewed by Agent Jones says that Joe Criminal could not have robbed the bank, because Joe Criminal was not in town on the day of the bank robbery. Must the government inform the defense about this witness?

A. yes, under Rule 17

B. yes, under the <u>Brady</u> doctrine

C. no, according to the Jencks Act

D. no, according to the 3rd Amendment

Answer: B. The <u>Brady</u> doctrine requires the government to inform the defense of any exculpatory information, whether or not requested by the defense.

---

31. Willy Doe is a witness for the government at trial. Willy Doe signed a statement to Special Agent Smith prior to testifying stating he saw the defendant commit the crime. Is the AUSA required to give the defense a copy of this statement?

A. yes, according to the Jencks Act

B. yes, according to *Brady*

C. no, because providing the statement violates the *Giglio* doctrine

D. no, because the defense is never able to obtain prior statements of government witnesses

Answer: A. The Jencks Act requires that the written, recorded, signed, or adopted statement of a government trial witness be given to the defense attorney no later than after the witness testifies on direct-examination for the government, but prior to cross-examination. The government could give the statement to the defense attorney at an earlier time if it wished. The judge could also order the statement be provided earlier. Because the statement does not appear to contain any exculpatory information, *Brady* doesn't apply. *Giglio* requires the government to give the defense possible impeachment evidence about witnesses the government may call. Answer D is simply not true - as we see by the correct answer, answer A.

---

32. Johnson lived in Little Rock, Arkansas his whole life. Johnson and some friends in Arkansas developed a hatred of the Federal government, and decided to blow up the Federal Building in Dallas, Texas. Johnson, with the help of his friends, actually went to Dallas and blew up the Federal Building. Following extensive investigation, Johnson is eventually arrested by Federal Agents in New York and charged with blowing up the Federal Building. Where must Johnson's trial for blowing up the Federal Building take place?

A. Johnson's trial must be held in New York.

B. Johnson's trial must be held in Dallas.

C. Johnson's trial must be held in Arkansas.

D. Johnson's trial could be held in any federal court.

Answer: D. The rules of venue state that the trial should be held in the District where the crime occurred. However, for good reason, the trial can be moved to another Federal Court in another District (change of venue). This is particularly true where the defendant is charged with a very horrible crime, creating a prejudice which prevents a fair trial in the District where the crime occurred.

––––––––––––––––––

33. In 1995, Joe stole 2 computers which were the property of the Federal government. The statute of limitations for this Federal crime is 5 years. Joe was indicted for this offense in 2001. Which of the following statements is correct?

A. Since it has been more than 5 years, Joe can't be prosecuted for this crime under any circumstances.

B. Since Joe stole 2 computers, the statute of limitations is 10 years, Joe can be prosecuted for the crime.

C. If Joe was indicted after 5 years, but prosecuted within 100 days of arrest, the Speedy Trial Act would permit his prosecution.

D. Joe could still be prosecuted if the 5 year statute of limitations was tolled by his concealing his identity or fleeing the jurisdiction to avoid prosecution.

Answer: D. If Joe fled or concealed his identity to avoid prosecution, the 5 year statute of limitations "clock" does not run during this time. Applicability of the statute of limitations is very case-specific. Therefore, Federal law enforcement officers should not drop a case based on the statute of limitations without first checking with the U.S. Attorney's office.

––––––––––––––––––

Federal Court Procedures Practice Exam

34. Who prepares the Pre-Sentencing Report used by the District Judge to determine the proper sentence for the Defendant?

A. the U.S. Probation Office with the help of the Federal law enforcement officer

B. the Clerk of Court with the help of the Federal law enforcement officer

C. the U.S. Probation Office with the help of the defense attorney

D. the Bailiff, with the help of the Clerk of Court

Answer: A. The Pre-Sentencing Report is prepared by the U.S. Probation Office with the help of the Federal law enforcement officer. The LEO should assist in providing such information.

---

35. Joe Smith robbed a bank in New York City. He is indicted and an arrest warrant is issued. Federal Agents arrest Joe Smith when they find him hiding in Cleveland, Ohio. Which of the following is a true statement about Joe Smith's case?

A. Smith's trial must be held in Cleveland, since that was the place of arrest.

B. Smith can choose whether to have his trial in Cleveland or New York.

C. Federal Agents should take Smith to New York without unnecessary delay for his initial appearance.

D. Once Smith is identified as the Joe Smith on the warrant, his case may be transferred to New York for trial.

Answer: D. Once it is established that the Joe Smith who has been arrested is the Joe Smith identified on the arrest warrant, the Court may transfer (remove) Smith's case to New York for further proceedings. This is the most common scenario, and the only correct choice above. It should be noted however, that if Smith wanted to waive his right to trial and plead guilty, his case could be resolved in Cleveland without transfer to New York.

Federal Court Procedures Practice Exam

36. Jacques Pierre, a citizen of France, is arrested by a federal agent in Jacksonville, Florida. Pierre is not a U.S. Citizen, but he has applied for citizenship and is expecting to complete the process within the next two to three months. Assume that France is not on the Vienna Convention on Consular Relations (VCCR) "mandatory notification countries" list. Which of the following actions must the arresting agent take?

A. He must notify the French Consulate of Pierre's arrest without delay.

B. He must offer, without delay, to notify Pierre's consular officials of the arrest.

C. He must determine the status of Pierre's citizenship application.

D. He must release Pierre because foreign nationals have diplomatic immunity.

Answer: B. The VCCR applies to all detentions and arrests of foreign nationals, so long as they are not U.S. citizens. The arrestee's immigration status is immaterial. In this case, because France is not on the VCCR "mandatory notification countries" list, the arresting officer is not required to immediately notify the French Consulate. Instead, the officer must offer to notify Pierre's consular officials of the arrest. Whether consular notification will be made depends upon Pierre's response. (As for answer D, there is nothing in the question to suggest that Pierre is a foreign diplomat. Not all foreign nationals are foreign diplomats or have diplomatic immunity.)

———————————

37. Austin Powers, a citizen of the United Kingdom, is arrested by a federal agent in Alexandria, VA, for selling unlicensed coffee mugs bearing the image of "Smokey Bear." Unlawful use of the "Smokey Bear" character or name is a federal misdemeanor (18 U.S.C. § 711). The United Kingdom is on the Vienna Convention on Consular Relations (VCCR) "mandatory notification countries" list. Is the arresting agent required to notify the British Consulate of Powers's arrest pursuant to the VCCR?

A. No, because the VCCR does not apply to misdemeanor offenses.

B. No, because the United Kingdom is an ally of the United States.

C. Yes, because the VCCR requires notification without delay to "mandatory notification countries."

D. Yes, but only if Powers immediately requests that his consular officials be notified.

Answer: C. The VCCR applies to all detentions and arrests of foreign nationals; the seriousness of the charge is immaterial. The VCCR requires, at a minimum, that the foreign national who is detained or arrested be told of the right to consular notification and access. In this case, because the United Kingdom is on the VCCR "mandatory notification countries" list, U.S. officials are required to notify the British Consulate of the arrest regardless of the arrestee's wishes.

———————————

Federal Court Procedures Practice Exam

38. The Vienna Convention on Consular Relations (VCCR) requires that foreign nationals who are detained or arrested in the U.S. be notified of:

A. the nature of the charges and their right to counsel

B. the right of consular notification and access

C. the right to remain silent and to refuse to sign any statements

D. the right to petition the U.S. Government for redress of grievances

Answer. B.   The VCCR requires that in all cases, a foreign national (non-U.S. citizen) arrested or detained within the United States be told of the right of consular notification and access. The rights described in answers A, C, and D, are protected by the Bill of Rights in the U.S. Constitution, not the VCCR.

———————————

39. Joe Youngster is a juvenile and has been arrested by federal officers. Which of the following is correct with respect to providing *Miranda* warnings before the officers attempt to question Joe?

A. Joe must be advised of his *Miranda* rights before questioning in words that a juvenile can understand.

B. Joe's parents or guardian, if they can be located through good faith efforts by law enforcement, must be advised of Joe's *Miranda* rights before questioning.

C, There is no requirement to advise Joe of his *Miranda* rights because he is a juvenile.

D. Both A and B.

Answer: D. In addition, law enforcement must also advise the parents or guardian of the alleged offense. If Joe's parents or guardian are located and they want to speak to Joe, that must be allowed. Remember also that law enforcement must not make the identity of the juvenile known publicly without prior approval of the district court.

———————————

Federal Court Procedures Practice Exam

Officer Liability Practice Exam

1. While on patrol, Sue ran up to Officer Smith. She looked battered and bruised. Sue pointed to a man approximately 20 feet away and said: "Help me officer, that man just attacked me!" Officer Smith then arrested the man, later identified at Johnson. Several weeks later, Sue admitted she had lied about being attacked by Johnson because she wanted attention. As a result, the charges against Johnson were dropped. Can Officer Smith be successfully sued for arresting Johnson?

a. Yes, because Officer Smith did not have probable cause to arrest Johnson.

b. Yes, since Johnson was not convicted.

c. No, because the information provided by Sue was probable cause to arrest Johnson.

d. No, because law enforcement officers are absolutely immune from being sued for any arrest they make.

Answer to question 1:

a. Yes, because Officer Smith did not have probable cause to arrest Johnson.
INCORRECT: Sue's appearance and statements establish probable cause for arrest.

b. Yes, since Johnson was not convicted.
INCORRECT: The standard for arrest is probable cause. The standard for conviction is proof beyond a reasonable doubt. Even if an individual is not later convicted, it does not mean that their arrest was improper. In this case, Sue's statements provide probable cause for a valid arrest.

c. No, because the information provided by Sue was probable cause to arrest Johnson.
CORRECT: Sue's statements provided probable cause to arrest. Officer Smith did nothing wrong in this case.

d. No, because law enforcement officers are absolutely immune from being sued for any arrest they make.
INCORRECT: Law enforcement officers are not absolutely immune from being sued. However, law enforcement officers receive qualified immunity from being sued for their actions. This means they are immune from suit for their actions as a law enforcement officer as long as they are acting as a reasonable law enforcement officer.

2. Two state police officers beat a handcuffed prisoner until he identified his drug supplier. The prisoner sued the officers. The lawsuit is legally recognized under:

a. the Federal Tort Claims Act

b. the Good Samaritan Act

c. *Bivens*

d. 42 U.S.C. 1983

Answer to question 2:

a. the Federal Tort Claims Act
INCORRECT: The FTCA is a law which allows the United States to be sued for the actions of federal employees committed within the scope of their employment. It does not apply to state or local police officers.

b. the Good Samaritan Act
INCORRECT: The federal Good Samaritan Act defines additional circumstances under which a federal officer might be determined to be in the scope of their employment. It does not apply to state or local police officers.

c. *Bivens*
INCORRECT: This would be correct if the two officers were federal agents, but *Bivens* does not authorize lawsuits against state or local officers.

d. 42 U.S.C. 1983
CORRECT: This statute authorizes civil lawsuits against state and local officials who violate federally protected rights.

3. Two federal agents illegally search Smith's house. The agents know they are conducting an illegal search, but they hope they will not get caught. Smith learns of the illegal search and sues the two federal agents. This lawsuit is legally recognized under:

a. the Federal Tort Claims Act

b. the Good Samaritan Act

c. *Bivens*

d. 42 U.S.C. 1983

Answer to question 3:

a. the Federal Tort Claims Act
INCORRECT: The FTCA is a law which allows the United States to be sued for the actions of federal employees committed within the scope of their employment. Knowingly conducting an illegal search is not an act within the scope of employment.

b. the Good Samaritan Act
INCORRECT: The federal Good Samaritan Act defines additional circumstances under which a federal officer might be determined to be in the scope of their employment. It does not apply to federal agents who are intentionally breaking the law.

c. *Bivens*
CORRECT: This case authorizes lawsuits against federal agents who intentionally violate an individual's 4th, 5th or 8th amendment rights.

d. 42 U.S.C. 1983
INCORRECT: This statute authorizes civil lawsuits against state and local officials who violate federally protected rights, not federal agents.

4. In a _Bivens_ action, a plaintiff must allege which of the following elements:

a. A federal law enforcement officer violated a Constitutional right while acting as a private citizen.

b. A federal law enforcement officer violated a Constitutional right while acting under color of law.

c. A state law enforcement officer violated a Constitutional right while acting as a private citizen.

d. A state law enforcement officer violated a Constitutional right while acting under color of law.

Answer to question 4:

a. A federal law enforcement officer violated a Constitutional right while acting as a private citizen.
INCORRECT: A _Bivens_ action is only appropriate if a Constitutional violation was committed by a federal officer acting under color of federal law. If an off-duty federal officer is simply acting as a private citizen, his actions cannot support a _Bivens_ lawsuit.

b. A federal law enforcement officer violated a Constitutional right while acting under color of law.
CORRECT: In a _Bivens_ action, the plaintiff must allege two elements: (1) A violation of a Constitutional right, and, (2) by a person acting under color of federal law.

c. A state law enforcement officer violated a Constitutional right while acting as a private citizen.
INCORRECT: A state law enforcement officer cannot be sued under _Bivens_. A state law enforcement officer could be sued under 42 U.S.C. Section 1983 for violating someone's rights while acting under color of state law. If an off-duty state officer is simply acting as a private citizen, his actions cannot support a 1983 lawsuit.

d. A state law enforcement officer violated a Constitutional right while acting under color of law.
INCORRECT: A state law enforcement officer cannot be sued under _Bivens_. A state law enforcement officer could be sued under 42 U.S.C. Section 1983 for violating someone's rights while acting under color of state law.

5. Smith was a federal agent who was authorized to drive a government vehicle 24 hours a day because of his duties. On his day off, he spotted some geese at his house that had been digging up his fancy landscaping. Attempting to scare the geese away from his lawn, he started his government vehicle and flashed his lights and siren. In his excitement, he accidentally put the car in drive and ran over his neighbor's mailbox. The neighbor can bring a successful lawsuit against which of the following:

a. Smith personally under *Bivens*

b. the U.S. Government under the FTCA

c. the U.S. Government under 42 U.S.C. 1983

d. Smith personally for negligence

Answer to question 5:

a. Smith personally under *Bivens*
INCORRECT: *Bivens* allows a lawsuit against an individual federal officer for violating someone's 4th, 5th, or 8th amendment rights while acting under color of law. Smith's actions didn't violate anyone's 4th, 5th or 8th amendment rights, and he wasn't acting under color of law.

b. Against the U.S. Government under the FTCA
INCORRECT: The U.S. Government is liable under the FTCA for actions by federal employees acting in the scope of their employment. Smith's actions were not in the scope of his employment.

c. Against the U.S. Government under 42 U.S.C. 1983
INCORRECT: This statute authorizes civil lawsuits against state and local officials who violate federally protected rights. Smith is a federal agent, and cannot be sued under this statute.

d. Against Smith personally for negligence
CORRECT: Since Smith was negligent, and not acting within the scope of his employment, the neighbor can file suit against Smith personally in state court.

6. Federal Officer Jones was driving his government car on the way to interview a witness to a crime under investigation. Jones became distracted, and ran into the back of Smith's car, causing $5000 worth of damage. In order to collect for his damages, 1) who should Smith sue, 2) in what court, and 3) who will pay the damages?

a. Smith should sue Jones in Federal court, and if Smith wins, Jones will pay the judgment.

b. Smith should sue Jones in Federal Court, but if the Smith wins, the United States will pay the judgment.

c. Smith should sue the United States in State court, and if Smith wins, the United States will pay the judgment.

d. Smith should sue the United States in Federal court, and if Smith wins, the United States will pay the judgment.

Answer to question 6:

a. Smith should sue Jones in Federal court, and if Smith wins, Jones will pay the judgment.
INCORRECT: See answer D.

b. Smith should sue Jones in Federal Court, but if the Smith wins, the United States will pay the judgment.
INCORRECT: See answer D.

c. Smith should sue the United States in State court, and if Smith wins, the United States will pay the judgment.
INCORRECT: See answer D.

d. Smith should sue the United States in Federal court, and if Smith wins, the United States will pay the judgment.
CORRECT: A federal employee acting in the scope of his employment is protected under the Federal Tort Claims Act. Therefore, if an employee injures someone while acting in the scope of their employment (meaning acting on behalf of the United States), the United States is the proper defendant under the Federal Tort Claims Act. The Federal Tort Claims Act also requires that the case will be tried in Federal District Court without a jury. The judge will decide if the United States is liable, and if so, for what amount. Additionally, there is a two year statute of limitations.

7. Officer Smith is watching Officer Jackson interview a prisoner. Convinced that the prisoner is lying to him, Officer Jackson hit and kicked the prisoner several times. Since this beating lasted several minutes, Officer Smith could have intervened and stopped the beating. However, Officer Smith decided to "mind his own business" and not get involved. The prisoner later sued both Officer Jackson and Officer Smith for the beating. Does Officer Smith have a valid defense to this lawsuit?

a. yes, the Federal Tort Claims Act

b. yes, qualified immunity

c. no, law enforcement officers can be sued whenever they fail to stop a crime

d. no, because he stood by while another officer violated the rights of an individual

Answer to question 7:

a. yes, the Federal Tort Claims Act
INCORRECT: The Federal Tort Claims Act protects federal employees from being sued for acts committed while they were acting within the scope of their employment. Officer Smith is not in the scope of his employment when he watches a fellow officer beat a prisoner without attempting to stop it.

b. yes, qualified immunity
INCORRECT: Qualified immunity is a defense from suit for any law enforcement officer who is acting as a reasonable law enforcement officer. Failing to intervene when a fellow officer is beating a suspect is not the behavior of a reasonable law enforcement officer.

c. no, law enforcement officers can be sued whenever they fail to stop a crime
INCORRECT: Ordinarily, there is no civil liability for failing to prevent crime or stop an ongoing crime. However, when a fellow officer is violating someone's civil rights, an officer has a duty to try and intervene.

d. no, because he stood by while another officer violated the rights of an individual
CORRECT: When a fellow officer is violating someone's civil rights, an officer has a duty to try and intervene.

8. A tort is a type of lawsuit where

a. the government prosecutes a citizen for a crime in the name of the government.

b. the government sues a citizen for having committed a crime.

c. a citizen sues another citizen for damages as a result of a negligent or intentional act.

d. a citizen prosecutes another citizen for damages as a result of a negligent or intentional act.

Answer to question 8:

a. the government prosecutes a citizen for a crime in the name of the government.
INCORRECT: This describes a criminal prosecution.

b. the government sues a citizen for having committed a crime.
INCORRECT: The word "sue" indicates a civil suit. The government does not sue people for committing a crime; they prosecute criminal offenders.

c. a citizen sues another citizen for damages as a result of a negligent or intentional act.
CORRECT: This is the definition of a tort action.

d. a citizen prosecutes another citizen for damages as a result of a negligent or intentional act.
INCORRECT: The word "prosecute" indicates a criminal prosecution. A criminal prosecution is not done in order to recover damages but to punish criminal misconduct.

9. Two federal agents are convinced Johnny is a drug smuggler, but they have no evidence. They agree to beat Johnny until he tells them where he hides his drugs. Johnny is never harmed and never learns of the plan. These agents could be prosecuted under:

a. 18 U.S.C. 241

b. 18 U.S.C. 242

c. *Bivens*

d. 42 U.S.C. 1983

Answer to question 9:

a. 18 U.S.C. 241
CORRECT: This is the federal criminal conspiracy against rights statute. When two or more agents conspire to deprive a citizen of constitutional rights, this is the appropriate statute to bring a criminal prosecution.

b. 18 U.S.C. 242
INCORRECT: This statute makes it a crime to violate someone's rights while acting "under color of law." Had the agents identified themselves and carried out their unlawful beating, they would also be guilty of this offense. However, since they never actually harmed Johnny, they cannot be arrested for this offense.

c. *Bivens*
INCORRECT: This statute authorizes civil lawsuits against federal officers who violate federally protected rights. It is not a criminal charge.

d. 42 U.S.C. 1983
INCORRECT: This statute authorizes civil lawsuits against state and local officials who violate federally protected rights. It is not a criminal charge.

10. Federal agent Adams is on duty when he sees Smith, the man who married his ex-wife. Still holding a grudge, Adams identifies himself as a federal agent and places Smith under arrest. Agent Adams has no legal reason to arrest Smith, so he just hits him a few times and then lets him go. Agent Adams could be prosecuted under:

a. 18 U.S.C. 241

b. 18 U.S.C. 242

c. *Bivens*

d. 42 U.S.C. 1983

Answer to question 10:

a. 18 U.S.C. 241
INCORRECT: This is the federal criminal conspiracy against rights statute. When two or more agents conspire to deprive a citizen of constitutional rights, this is the appropriate statute to bring a criminal prosecution. However, since Agent Adams acted alone, it is not appropriate in this case.

b. 18 U.S.C. 242
CORRECT: This statute makes it a crime to violate someone's rights while acting "under color of law." Since Agent Adams abused his authority and made this unlawful arrest, he is subject to prosecution for this offense.

c. *Bivens*
INCORRECT: This statute authorizes civil lawsuits against federal officers who violate federally protected rights. It is not a criminal charge.

d. 42 U.S.C. 1983
INCORRECT: This statute authorizes civil lawsuits against state and local officials who violate federally protected rights. It is not a criminal charge.

Officer Liability Practice Exam